DK EYEWITNESS

T0001570

TOP 10
MADRID

Top 10 Madrid Highlights

The Top 10 of Everything

CONTENTS

Madrid Area by Area

Streetsmart

Within each Top 10 list in this book, no hierarchy of quality or popularity is implied. All 10 are, in the editor's opinion, of roughly equal merit.

Title page, front cover and spine *The stunning Catedral de la Almudena in Madrid*
Back cover, clockwise from top left *Spanish tapas; Edificio Metrópolis, Gran Vía; lush Parque del Retiro; Catedral de la Almudena; Toledo street, Plaza Mayor*

The rapid rate at which the world is changing is constantly keeping the DK Eyewitness team on our toes. While we've worked hard to ensure that this edition of Madrid is accurate and up-to-date, we know that opening hours alter, standards shift, prices fluctuate, places close and new ones pop up in their stead. So, if you notice we've got something wrong or left something out, we want to hear about it. Please get in touch at **travelguides@dk.com**

Welcome to
Madrid

Located right in the heart of Spain, Madrid's attractions include world-class art, a lavish royal palace, glorious gardens and showpiece squares. It's a place that fizzes with energy and creativity, yet preserves plenty of old-fashioned appeal. Contemporary art, dance and theatre thrive, while traditional festivals bring *Madrileños* out in droves. With DK Eyewitness Top 10 Madrid, it's yours to explore.

For all of Madrid's big-city bustle, it still feels surprisingly intimate, thanks to the appeal of its different districts, and the friendliness of its inhabitants. Swanky **Salamanca** has the fanciest restaurants and boutiques, while **La Latina** is home to **Mercado de la Cebada**, which sells fresh produce, and atmospheric tapas bars. Gritty **Lavapiés** is great for vintage stores and underground bars, while boho-chic **Chueca**'s cocktail bars and cafés feature regularly in glossy magazines.

You can walk in the footsteps of great writers in the **Barrio de las Letras**; visit the majestic **Palacio Real**, the largest royal palace in Western Europe; or watch the sun set over the **Guadarrama mountains**. Shiver at Picasso's *Guernica* in the **Museo Nacional Centro de Arte Reina Sofía**, and try to interpret the enigmatic smile of the *Lady of Elche* in the **Archaeological Museum**. Once night falls, don't forget that *Madrileños* (locals) aren't known as *gatos* (cats) for nothing: you'll dine and party late in this city that never sleeps.

Whether you are visiting for a weekend or a week, our Top 10 guide brings together the best of everything the city has to offer, from Goya's "Black Paintings" in the **Prado** to almond blossoms in the **Parque Quinta de los Molinos**. The guide has useful tips throughout, from seeking out what's free to places off the beaten track, plus nine easy-to-follow itineraries, designed to tie together a clutch of sights in a short space of time. Add inspiring photography and detailed maps, and you've got the essential pocket-sized travel companion. **Enjoy the book, and enjoy Madrid.**

Clockwise from top: The majestic Palacio de Cibeles, Old Madrid café, Catedral de la Almudena, park with almond blossoms, Museo Nacional Centro de Arte Reina Sofía, bridge over Río Manzanares

Exploring Madrid

Madrid packs in a fantastic array of historic museums and monuments, parks and gardens, plus great shopping, dining and nightlife. You'll be spoiled for choice whatever your interests and however long you spend in the city. Here are some ideas for two and four days of sightseeing and fun in beautiful Madrid.

Plaza Mayor is the city's grandest and most famous square.

Key
— Two-day itinerary
— Four-day itinerary

Two Days in Madrid

Day ❶
MORNING
Enjoy a coffee on the **Plaza Mayor** *(see pp22–3)*, Madrid's showcase square, before strolling east to the Paseo del Prado and the magnificent **Museo Nacional del Prado** *(see pp16–21)*. There's too much to see in one visit, so select some highlights.

AFTERNOON
After lunch, head to **Parque del Retiro** *(see pp36–7)* to stroll through the beautiful gardens, before walking down to the **Museo Nacional Centro de Arte Reina Sofía** *(see pp32–5)* to admire its collection of modern art.

Day ❷
MORNING
Visit the splendid 19th-century **Palacio de Gaviria** *(see p96)*, which features ceiling paintings, chandeliers and gilt mirrors. It regularly hosts changing art exhibitions. Then stop at the **Mercado de San Miguel** *(see p105)* for lunch.

AFTERNOON
Sip a coffee on the handsome **Plaza de Oriente** *(see p103)*, before heading into the **Palacio Real** *(see pp12–15)*, one of the largest palaces in Europe.

Four Days in Madrid

Day ❶
MORNING
Head out early to Madrid's biggest attraction, the **Museo Nacional del Prado** *(see pp16–21)*. Spend the morning taking in the fine collection of European artworks, and be sure to look out for Goya's "Black Paintings", or *Las Meninas* by Velázquez.

AFTERNOON
Amble through the narrow streets of Madrid's historic heart to the elegant **Plaza Mayor** *(see pp22–3)*, then visit the beautiful **Palacio Gaviria** *(see p96)*, known for its fabulous art exhibitions.

Day ❷
MORNING
Spend a morning with the enigmatic *Lady of Elche* and other archaeological gems at the **Museo**

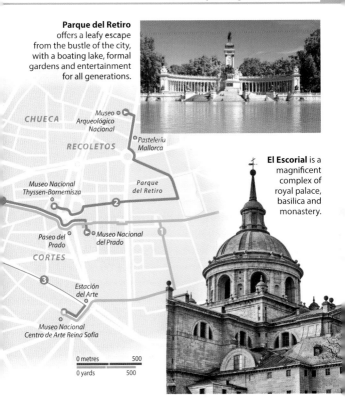

Parque del Retiro offers a leafy escape from the bustle of the city, with a boating lake, formal gardens and entertainment for all generations.

CHUECA

Museo Arqueológico Nacional

RECOLETOS

Pastelería Mallorca

Museo Nacional Thyssen-Bornemisza

Parque del Retiro

El Escorial is a magnificent complex of royal palace, basilica and monastery.

Paseo del Prado

Museo Nacional del Prado

CORTES

Estación del Arte

Museo Nacional Centro de Arte Reina Sofía

| 0 metres | 500 |
| 0 yards | 500 |

Arqueológico Nacional (see pp38–9). Then pick up some picnic goodies, perhaps at **Pastelería Mallorca** (see p88), and head for the gardens of the **Parque del Retiro** (see pp36–7).

AFTERNOON

The early Italian Madonnas and works by the French Impressionists provide soothing company at the **Museo Nacional Thyssen-Bornemisza** (see pp28–31). The garden café is an idyllic spot for refreshment and rest.

Day ❸

MORNING

If you're in Madrid on a Sunday, make an early visit to the El Rastro flea market (see pp26–7). Spend the rest of the morning in the extravagant **Palacio Real** (see pp12–15), whose gilded salons are decorated with exquisite paintings and tapestries.

AFTERNOON

Visit the **Museo Nacional Centro de Arte Reina Sofía** (see pp32–5) to admire Picasso's masterpiece, *Guernica*, along with works by Dalí, Miró, Gris, and contemporary artists including Eduardo Arroyo and Miquel Barceló.

Day ❹

MORNING AND AFTERNOON

Spend the whole day at the splendid royal monastery, basilica and palace complex of **El Escorial** (see pp40–43). Between admiring the surprisingly simple apartments, the ornate basilica and the magnificent library, head for the glorious gardens to enjoy a picnic (if you come prepared), or a late lunch afterwards at one of the restaurants in San Lorenzo de El Escorial (see pp130–31).

Top 10 Madrid Highlights

Boating lake and monument to Alfonso XII at Parque del Retiro

🔟 Madrid Highlights

Madrid's three world-class art museums and two royal palaces alone would set pulses racing, but there is more to this exciting and diverse capital than its tourist sights, from the high-fashion boutiques of Salamanca to Madrid's world-famous tapas. Head for the supremely elegant Plaza Mayor to simply watch the world go by.

1 Palacio Real

Once the residence of Spain's Bourbon rulers, there's something here for everyone (see pp12–15).

2 Museo Nacional del Prado

This world-famous gallery, with outstanding collections, is Madrid's must-see (see pp16–21).

3 Plaza Mayor

A magnificent square, now lined with shops, this plaza has been the focal point of the city for centuries (see pp22–3).

4 Real Basílica de San Francisco el Grande

Built in the 18th century, this church is full of outstanding works of art and features a huge dome decorated with brightly coloured frescoes (see pp24–5).

5 El Rastro

Find unique treasures at one of Madrid's most famous open-air flea markets, which can trace its roots back more than 400 years (see pp26–7).

7 Museo Nacional Centro de Arte Reina Sofía

No visitor should miss Picasso's *Guernica*, the famous 20th-century painting. The museum also showcases many other modern Spanish greats *(see pp32–5)*.

6 Museo Nacional Thyssen-Bornemisza

This priceless collection of 13th–20th century European art attracts nearly a million visitors every year *(see pp28–31)*.

Parque del Retiro 8

Once the preserve of royalty, this park is now enjoyed by visitors and *Madrileños* alike *(see pp36–7)*.

9 Museo Arqueológico Nacional

This vast archaeological museum is home to over 300,000 dazzling art-works and artifacts, now displayed to best effect in a superbly renovated setting *(see pp38–9)*.

10 El Escorial

Set against the stunning backdrop of the Sierra de Guadarrama mountains, Felipe II's awe-inspiring palace, basilica and monastery complex was founded as a mausoleum for Spain's Habsburg rulers *(see pp40–43)*.

🔟 ⭐ Palacio Real

Madrid's fabulous Royal Palace is one of Europe's outstanding architectural monuments. More than half of the state apartments are open to the public, sumptuously decorated with silk wall hangings, frescoes and gilded stucco, and crammed with priceless objets d'art. The palace's setting is equally breathtaking: beyond the main courtyard (Plaza de la Armería) lies an uninterrupted vista of park and woodland, stretching to the majestic peaks of the Sierra de Guadarrama.

Façade **1**

Stand for a few moments on Plaza de Oriente to enjoy the splendour of Sacchetti's façade **(right)**, gleaming in the sun. Sacchetti achieved a rhythm by alternating Ionic columns with Tuscan pilasters.

3 Hall of Columns

Once the setting for balls and banquets, this room is still used for ceremonial occasions, with Giaquinto's fresco of Carlos III (shown as the sun god Apollo) and superb 17th-century silk tapestries.

2 Main Staircase

When Napoleon first saw the exquisite frescoes **(above)** on the staircase after installing his brother on the Spanish throne, he said, "Joseph, your lodgings will be better than mine."

4 Throne Room

This room **(right)** was designed for Charles III by Giovanni Battista Natali as a glorification of the monarchy. The bronze lions by the throne were made in Rome in 1651.

NEED TO KNOW

MAP J3 ■ Calle Bailén
■ 914 54 88 00 ■ www.
patrimonionacional.es

Open Apr–Sep: 10am–8pm daily (Oct–Mar: to 6pm; 24 & 31 Dec: to 3pm); closed 1 & 6 Jan, 1 May & 25 Dec

Adm €13, €7 (concessions), additional €4 for guided tour and €3 for audio guide; free Mon–Thu (Apr–Sep: 6–8pm; Oct–Mar: 4–6pm); free for under-5s, EU citizens & Ibero-Americans

■ The palace can close for official ceremonies without prior warning; check ahead. Avoid queues by arriving early in the morning.

■ On the first Wed (Oct–Jul), see the grand Changing of the Guard ceremony at noon. On all other Wed and Sat, there's a ceremony from 11am–2pm.

■ The avenue in Jardines del Campo del Moro (see p52) offers great views of the palace's façade.

7 Gasparini Room

Named after its Italian creator, this magnificent room **(left)** was Charles III's robing room. The beautiful ceiling is encrusted with stuccoed fruit and flowers and is an excellent example of 18th-century *chinoiserie*.

BUILDING THE PALACE

This palace stands on the site of the Alcázar, the 9th-century Moorish fortress. The wooden structure burned down in 1734 and Felipe V initially commissioned Italian architect Filippo Juvarra, then Giovanni Sacchetti, to design a replacement. Work began in 1738 and was completed in 1764. However, the present King Felipe VI prefers to live at the Palacio de la Zarzuela outside the city.

5 The Royal Kitchens

Set in the basement of the palace, these kitchens were designed in 1737. The wedding feast of King Felipe VI and Queen Letizia was prepared here. Known to be the oldest, most well-preserved royal kitchens in Europe, they display 2,625 utensils, bearing the royal crest.

8 The Royal Library

Founded in 1712 by King Felipe V, the Royal Library contains more than 20,000 articles, including Isabel I of Castile's *Book of Hours*, a Bible which belonged to Doña María de Molina. There is a volume of Scriptures from the era of Alfonso XI of Castile as well.

9 Armoury

Housed in a pavilion built in 1897, the royal armoury has more than 2,000 pieces, mostly made for jousts and tournaments rather than for the battlefield. It also has instruments of torture dating from the days of the Spanish Inquisition.

10 Royal Chapel

Ventura Rodríguez is usually credited with the decoration of this chapel, although he worked hand-in-hand with other collaborators. The dome, supported by massive columns of black marble, is illuminated with more of Giaquinto's frescoes.

6 Gala Dining Room

The banqueting hall **(right)** was created for the wedding of Alfonso XII in 1879. The tapestries and ceiling frescoes are by Anton Mengs and Diego Velázquez. Look out for the Chinese vases "of a thousand flowers" in the window recesses.

Art Treasures in the Palacio Real

 Boabdil's Dagger
This beautiful jewelled dagger in the Armoury belonged to the 15th-century Muslim ruler Muhammad XII, who was also known as Boabdil.

 Vertumnus and Pomona Tapestries
These exquisite tapestries in the Gala Dining Room were made in Brussels by Willem de Pannemaker in the mid-16th century.

3 **Porcelain**
Among the royal porcelain are some fine examples of Sèvres and Meissen dinnerware.

Tapestry of St John, Hall of Columns

 Tapestries in the Hall of Columns
These 16th-century tapestries depict scenes from the lives of the Apostles.

5 **Goya Portraits**
The quartet of portraits by Goya, depicting Carlos IV and his wife Maria Luisa, shows the queen as a Spanish *maja* (beauty).

6 **Table of the Sphinxes**
This 18th-century piece in the Hall of Columns has six bronze sphinxes as table supports.

7 **Chronos Clock**
Made for Carlos IV in 1799, this clock contains a marble sculpture of Chronos, representing time.

Violin made by Antonio Stradivari

8 **Stradivarius Violins**
The priceless "Palace Quartet" (two violins, a viola and violoncello) was made in the 18th century by the world-famous luthier, Antonio Stradivari.

9 **Giaquinto's Apollo**
Corrado Giaquinto's fresco on the ceiling of the Hall of Columns depicts Carlos III as the sun god Apollo, riding in his chariot across the heavens.

10 **Grandeur and Power of the Spanish Monarchy**
Giovanni Battista Tiepolo's frescoes in the Throne Room are a *tour de force*. Marginal figures represent Spain's overseas possessions.

Tiepolo's frescoes, Throne Room

THE HABSBURGS AND THE BOURBONS

The Austrian house of Habsburg ruled Spain for nearly 200 years (1516–1700), beginning with Carlos I (Emperor Charles V) and his son Felipe II *(see p43)*. By the time the first Bourbon king, Felipe V (grandson of Louis XIV of France), came to the throne, Spain was already in decline. Felipe was immediately challenged by the Habsburg Archduke Charles of Austria, causing the disastrous War of the Spanish Succession (1701–14) which led to Spain losing territories in Italy, Belgium, Sardinia, Luxembourg and Gibraltar. The presence of the Bourbons gave Napoleon an excuse to interfere in Spanish affairs, eventually imposing his brother as king. Although the Bourbons were restored (1814), more than a century of political turmoil followed. At this time the dynasty's right to rule was continually challenged until the monarchy was abolished in 1931. After the death of dictator General Franco, in 1975, his nominated successor, the Bourbon King Juan Carlos I, presided over the restoration of democracy, until he abdicated in favour of his son Felipe VI in June 2014.

Carlos III, an admired and successful ruler

TOP 10 HABSBURG AND BOURBON RULERS

1 **Carlos I** (1516–56)
2 **Felipe II** (1556–98)
3 **Felipe III** (1598–1621)
4 **Felipe V** (1724–46)
5 **Carlos III** (1759–88)
6 **Carlos IV** (1788–1808)
7 **Fernando VII** (1813–33)
8 **Isabel II** (1833–68)
9 **Alfonso XIII** (1902–31)
10 **Juan Carlos I** (1975–2014)

The Battle of Turin, 1706, by Joseph Parrocel; a key point in the War of the Spanish Succession

🔟 ⭐ Museo Nacional del Prado

One of the world's finest art galleries, the Prado has at its core the Royal Collection of mainly 16th- and 17th-century paintings. Its strongest suit is Spanish painting: artists include Goya with 114 paintings on display, and Velázquez with 50. The Italian collection includes masterpieces by Fra Angelico, Raphael, Botticelli, Titian and Tintoretto. The Prado owns more than 90 works by Rubens, and canvases by leading Flemish and Dutch artists. A wing designed by Spanish architect Rafael Moneo, in the Jerónimos Monastery, hosts temporary exhibitions and Renaissance sculpture from the permanent collection. The north attic was reopened in 2018, allowing room for 1,700 works.

1 St Dominic Presiding over an Auto-de-Fé
Spanish artist Pedro Berruguete (c.1445–1503) was influenced by the Italians. This painting from around 1495 shows St Dominic sitting in judgment with members of the Inquisition.

2 The Adoration of the Shepherds
Born in Crete, El Greco (1541–1614) was given his nickname ("The Greek") after settling in Toledo in 1577. This inspirational 1612 masterpiece **(above)** was intended for his own tomb.

3 Jacob's Dream
José de Ribera (1591-1652) reveals his mastery in Jacob's Dream **(right)**, a painting relating to Jacob the Patriarch's mysterious dream as told in Genesis. This artwork (c.1639) displays José's excellent compositional ability and his delicate sense of colour.

4 Nude Maja
This famous portrait (c.1795–1800) by Francisco Goya (1746–1828) is one of the rare examples of a nude in a Spanish painting of the time. It is one of a pair – the *Clothed Maja* is in the same room for comparison.

5 Holy Family with Little Bird
Like his contemporary Francisco de Zurbarán, Bartolomé Esteban Murillo (1617–82) worked in and around Seville, mainly in the decoration of convents and monasteries. This beautiful work (1650), painted with fluent brushstrokes, is typical of his style.

6 Las Meninas
This virtuoso exercise in perspective (1656) is by Diego Velázquez (1599–1660). Flanking the Infanta Margarita **(below)** are two ladies-in-waiting *(las Meninas)*. The scene also includes the artist, with paintbrush and palette in hand.

7 **The Spinners**
This painting **(above)** (c.1657) by Velázquez is an allegory based on the legend of the weaver Arachne.

8 **St Jerome**
José de Ribera (1591–1652) painted this 1615 depiction of St Jerome in 1644. Like many Spanish artists of the period, Ribera was influenced by Caravaggio.

9 **The Meadow of St Isidore**
This 1788 Goya landscape brilliantly evokes the atmosphere of the San Isidro celebrations (see p74) and the clear light of spring.

10 **The Third of May 1808: The Shootings on Príncipe Pío Hill**
In this dramatic 1814 painting, Goya captures the execution of the leaders of the ill-fated insurrection against the French. The illuminated, Christ-like figure (see p19) represents the spirit of freedom being mowed down by the forces of oppression.

NEED TO KNOW

MAP F5 ■ Paseo del Prado ■ 913 30 28 00; for advance tickets call 910 68 30 01 ■ www.museodelprado.es

Open 10am–8pm Mon–Sat (to 7pm Sun & public hols; 6 Jan, 24 & 31 Dec: to 2pm); closed 1 Jan, 1 May & 25 Dec

Adm €15, €7.50 (concessions); adm & guide book €24; free 6–8pm Mon–Sat, 5–7pm Sun & public hols

■ Tickets must be purchased in advance; it is recommended to buy tickets online or by phone.

■ For disabled access, use the Los Jerónimos entrance.

■ Works of art may change location and some parts of the museum may be temporarily closed. Check the website or call the information telephone number before visiting.

■ There's a museum shop, restaurant and café; food cannot be brought in from outside the museum.

MUSEUM GUIDE

In the Villanueva Building, the second floor has paintings from 1700 to 1800; the first floor has paintings from 1550 to 1810; the ground floor has paintings from 1100 to 1910 and sculptures; decorative arts are in the basement. The Jerónimos Building has sculptures and temporary exhibitions. The locations of the paintings may shift so pick up a floorplan on arrival.

Museo Nacional del Prado Floorplan

Key to Floorplan
■ Second floor
■ First floor
■ Ground floor

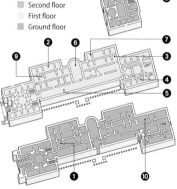

Italian Paintings in the Prado

Death of the Virgin **by Mantegna**

Italian Paintings Floorplan

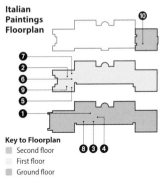

Key to Floorplan
- Second floor
- First floor
- Ground floor

1 Death of the Virgin
This 1460 painting by Andrea Mantegna (c.1431–1506) depicts the last moments of the Virgin Mary's life.

2 Madonna and Child between Two Saints
Founder of the Venetian School, Giovanni Bellini (c.1431–1516) shows an assured use of colour in this devotional painting (c.1490).

3 The Story of Nastagio degli Onesti
These panels (1483) by Botticelli (c.1444–1510) were commissioned by two rich Florentine families.

4 Portrait of a Cardinal
This painting (c.1510) by Raphael (1483–1520) is notable for its striking colour palette.

5 Christ Washing the Disciples' Feet
This early work (1547) by Jacopo Tintoretto (c.1518–94) reveals his brilliant handling of perspective.

6 Danaë and the Shower of Gold
Paintings by Titian (1488–1576) were prized by Carlos I. This 1553 work depicts a mythological story by Ovid.

7 David with the Head of Goliath
Caravaggio (1571–1610) had a major impact on Spanish artists, who admired the dark and light contrasts, as seen here (c.1600).

8 Annunciation and The Virgin with the Pomegranate
This work (c.1428) by Fra Angelico (c.1400–55) is third in the series of panels. Prado Museum acquired this from the Alba Ducal collection.

9 Venus and Adonis
This beautiful work (c.1580) by Paolo Veronese (1528–88) is a masterpiece of light and colour.

Venus and Adonis **by Paolo Veronese**

10 The Immaculate Conception
This work (1767–9) by Giambattista Tiepolo (1696–1770) is one of a series intended for a church in Aranjuez.

GOYA'S "BLACK PAINTINGS"

Portrait of Francisco Goya

Technically brilliant, satirical, sarcastic and bitter, Goya's "Black Paintings", exhibited in room 67 on the ground floor of the Villanueva Building, are some of the most extraordinary works in the history of art. They originally decorated the rooms of his house, the *Quinta del Sordo* (Villa of the Deaf), near the Manzanares River and were produced while he was recovering from a serious illness. In 1873, the then owner of the *Quinta*, Baron d'Erlanger, had the paintings transferred to canvas and donated them to the Prado Museum. What these 14 paintings have in common, apart from the uniformly sombre colour scheme, is a preoccupation with corruption, human misery, sickness and death. The key to the series is the terrifying *Saturn Devouring his Son*, which is based on a painting by Rubens, but in which the god is transformed from a Baroque hero to the incarnation of evil. Even *San Isidro Fair,* which features Goya himself, is almost a travesty of his earlier depiction of the festival *(see p17)*, and reveals how far he had travelled as man and artist over the years.

TOP 10 EVENTS IN THE LIFE OF FRANCISCO DE GOYA

1 Born in Fuendetodos, near Zaragoza (1746)

2 Joined workshop of local artist, José Luzán (1760)

3 Moved to Madrid and worked at Royal Tapestry Factory (1774)

4 Admitted to San Fernando Academy (1780)

5 Appointed court painter (1786)

6 Lost his hearing (1792)

7 Began an affair with Duchess of Alba (c.1796)

8 Witnessed failed uprising against the French (1808)

9 Went into exile in France (1824)

10 Died in Bordeaux (1828)

The Third of May 1808: The Shootings on Príncipe Pío Hill, **Francisco Goya**

Flemish and Dutch Paintings

Flemish and Dutch Paintings Floorplan

Key to Floorplan
First floor
Ground floor

The Descent from the Cross

1 The Descent from the Cross

Felipe II hung this beautiful composition (c.1435) by Rogier van der Weyden (1399–1464) in El Escorial (see pp40–43). It was moved here after the Civil War.

2 The Garden of Delights

The meaning of this famous and unsettling work (1500) by Hieronymus Bosch (c.1450–1516) is hotly debated. The traditional view is that it is a warning against earthly pleasures.

3 The Triumph of Death

This terrifying version of the Dance of Death (c.1562–3) is by Flemish master, Pieter Breughel the Elder (c.1525–69).

4 Portrait of Mary Tudor

Antonis Mor (1517–76) painted this superb portrait in 1554 of the 37-year-old Queen of England, who was to marry Felipe II.

5 Judith at the Banquet of Holofernes

This 1634 painting is the only work in the Prado by Rembrandt (1606–69). Judith's maid can be seen carrying the sack into which Judith will later place the head of her enemy, Holofernes.

The Three Graces by Peter Paul Rubens

6 The Painter's Family

Jacob Jordaens (1593–1678) was one of the finest portrait artists of the 17th century, as can be seen in this 1622 painting of himself with his wife and daughter. The painting is full of symbols of marital fidelity.

7 The Artist with Sir Endymion Porter

This double portrait painted from 1632–7 by Anthony van Dyck (1599–1641) shows him with the diplomat Endymion Porter, his friend and patron at the court of King Charles I.

8 Adoration of the Magi

Peter Paul Rubens (1577–1640) first painted this in 1609 but returned to it in 1628 to add three strips that included various figures and his self-portrait.

9 Landscape with Saint Jerome

This 1516–17 Joachim Patenier (1480–1524) work depicts the saint gently removing a thorn from the paw of a lion.

10 The Three Graces

This erotic masterpiece (c.1635) by Rubens was inspired by classical sculpture. It features Love, Desire and Virginity, two of whom were modelled on the artist's wives.

FURTHER EUROPEAN HIGHLIGHTS IN THE PRADO

Self Portrait by Albrecht Dürer, painted in 1498

The highlights of the small but valuable German Collection (room 55B ground floor) are Albrecht Dürer's *Self Portrait*, painted in 1498, one of a quartet of paintings by this Renaissance master, and his depictions of Adam and Eve. Most of the French Collection dates from the 17th and 18th centuries (first floor, rooms 2–4). The landscapes of Claude Lorrain and the work of Nicolas Poussin are outstanding. Felipe II began collecting Classical sculptures (ground floor, rooms 71–4) in the 16th century, mostly Roman copies of Greek originals. Look out for the three Venuses – *Madrid Venus, Venus with a Shell, Venus of the Dolphin* – and the priceless San Ildefonso Group, dating from the reign of the Emperor Augustus (1st century AD). The Dauphin's Treasure (basement) was inherited by Felipe V, heir presumptive to Louis XIV of France. The fabulous collection of goblets, glasses and serving dishes was made from precious stones (jasper, lapis lazuli, agate and rock crystal) and encrusted with jewels.

TOP 10 EUROPEAN WORKS OF ART

1 Self Portrait, Albrecht Dürer (German Collection)

2 Hunt at the Castle of Torgau in Honour of Charles V, Lucas Cranach the Elder (German Collection)

3 St Paula Romana Embarking at Ostia, Claude Lorrain (French Collection)

4 Parnassus, Nicolas Poussin (French Collection)

5 San Ildefonso statues (Classical Sculptures)

6 Madrid Venus (Classical Sculptures)

7 Venus with a Shell (Classical Sculptures)

8 Statue of Demeter (Classical Sculptures)

9 Onyx salt cellar with Mermaid (Dauphin's Treasure)

10 The Hunt Vessel (Dauphin's Treasure)

Parnassus **by Nicolas Poussin (1594–1665)**

TOP 10 ⭐ Plaza Mayor

Madrid's most famous square, completed in 1619, was built on a grand scale. Capable of holding up to 50,000 people, it was intended to impress, and still does. Nowadays it's a tourist attraction first and foremost: a place for relaxing with a drink amid the bustle of tour groups and sightseers. It was originally known as Plaza del Arrabal ("Outskirts Square") because it lay outside the city walls. Following a fire in 1791, Juan de Villanueva (architect of the Prado) redesigned the square, adding the granite archways that now enclose it. Plaza Mayor has been a market, an open-air theatre, a bullring and a place of execution. Its buildings are now mainly used by the city government.

1 Statue of Felipe III

The large statue by two Italian artists, Pietro Tacca and Giambologna, was moved to the centre of this square in the 19th century. Presented to Felipe III in 1616 by the Florentine ruler Cosimo de' Medici, it was originally in the Casa de Campo.

2 Casa de la Panadería

The headquarters of the bakers' guild, this house had great power in controlling the price of grain. The portal still survives from the original building which burned down in 1672.

3 Arco de Cuchilleros

Cutlers Arch is so called for the sword-makers who once traded here. Today the street is known for taverns such as Las Cuevas de Luis Candelas, named after a 19th-century bandit said to have hidden in its cellars.

The grand Plaza Mayor

4 Casa de la Panadería Murals

In the 1980s it was decided that the façade murals of "Bakery House" were beyond saving, and a competition was held for a new design. The winner, Carlos Franco, painted allegories of the zodiac signs **(left)** in 1992.

5 Casa de la Carnicería

This building on the south side of Plaza Mayor was erected in 1617 and was originally the meat market. It is now used by the Junta Municipal del Distrito de Centro (Central District Government).

NEED TO KNOW
MAP M5

■ Stock up in the nearby Mercado de San Miguel *(see p71)* for a picnic on one of the square's benches. Try a calamari sandwich, a Madrid speciality.

■ The painted enamel street signs, for which Madrid is famous, provide a clue to the original inhabitants, such as Calle de los Botoneros (Button-makers' Street).

■ One of the city's main tourist offices *(915 78 78 10)* can be found at Plaza Mayor 27.

6 Arcade Shops

Buying and selling has always been the lifeblood of Plaza Mayor, with shops **(above)** selling everything from espadrilles to icons. At El Arco Artesanía (No. 9), all the items on sale have been made by local artisans, continuing a centuries-old tradition.

Cava de San Miguel 7

When the houses were built on this street **(right)** adjacent to Plaza Mayor, huge quantities of earth were removed from the foundations of the square. To prevent its collapse, frontages on the Cava were designed as sloping buttresses.

9 Terrace Bars and Cafés

Relaxing over a leisurely drink on an outdoor terrace is the best way to appreciate the square. Look out for the speciality *bocadillo de calamares* (bread roll filled with fried squid).

10 Stamp and Coin Market

This market takes place every Sunday morning from around 10am to 2pm and attracts amateur and expert collectors from all over Spain.

8 Lampposts

The modern lampposts **(left)** set around the statue of Felipe III are engraved with scenes depicting life on the square in days gone by. They include a masquerade ball, an interrogation by members of the Inquisition and a bullfight.

AUTO-DE-FÉ

The cellars at No. 4 of Calle Felipe III were once used by the Inquisition to torture those accused of heresy, witchcraft and a multitude of other crimes. The condemned had to undergo a ceremony known as the auto-de-fé. This macabre spectacle, which included a ritual procession and public humiliation, lasted from dawn to dusk.

TOP 10 ⭐ Real Basílica de San Francisco el Grande

Richly endowed with the work of great artists, the Real Basílica de San Francisco el Grande is one of Madrid's most iconic churches. The focal point of its unusual circular design is the stupendous dome – the biggest in Spain and the fourth largest in Europe – which was designed by Francisco Cabezas but completed, after work was halted due to complications with the size, by Francesco Sabatini in 1784. The basilica was declared a National Monument in 1980 and now, after 30 years of restoration, its ceiling frescoes are once again revealed in their original glory.

1 The Dome

One of the basilica's most striking features, the immense dome **(right)** measures 58 m (190 ft) high and 33 m (108 ft) in diameter. A work of art in itself, it is divided into eight main panels decorated with majestic frescoes depicting scenes of kings and saints paying homage to the Virgin Mary.

2 The Doors

The seven main doors leading inside were carved in walnut in the 19th century by architect Casa Juan Guas. Some of the finest relief work can be seen on the three central doors, depicting Christ crucified and, to either side, Dismas and Gestas, the thieves who died alongside Him.

3 The Exterior

Following a renovation project in 1878, the basilica's Neo-Classical façade **(left)** is dominated by the dome and twin towers. Its simple decoration, featuring Doric columns on the lower level and slender Ionic columns on the upper, is the work of the royal architect Francesco Sabatini.

NEED TO KNOW

MAP B5 ■ Calle Gran Vía de San Francisco 19
■ 913 65 38 00

Open 8–10:30am Mon–Sat (closed during services on Sat), 10am–1:30pm & 6:30–8pm Sun

Adm €5; concessions €3

■ Café Delic *(see p116)*, located on picturesque Plaza de la Paja, is a short walk up Calle de Bailén and Calle de la Redondilla.

■ A guided tour (Tue–Fri) of the basilica is included in the admission fee. The tour is in Spanish, but the guides are happy to answer questions in English.

4 The Side Chapels

The six side chapels **(above)** feature large frescoes. Look out for Mariano Salvador Maella's *Immaculate Conception* (1784) and José Casado del Alisal's *Santiago at the Battle of Clavijo* (1885).

5 The Nave

The basilica's nave is unusual in that it is circular in shape and is positioned directly beneath the dome, where the altar is normally located.

6 The 12 Apostles

Marble sculptures of the 12 Apostles guard the side chapels' entrances. They were made by many artists, including Agapit Vallmitjana i Barbany and Jerónimo Suñol.

7 The Galleries

Behind the High Altar, several corridors display artwork from the 17th to 19th centuries, many depicting the life of St Francis of Assisi. According to legend, the basilica occupies the site of a convent founded by the saint in 1217.

8 Capilla de San Bernadino

The chapel of San Bernardino de Siena features one of Francisco Goya's most stunning paintings, *San Bernadino de Siena Preaching Before Alfonso V of Aragón* (1784). It depicts a rare self-portrait of the artist (he's in the yellow tunic on the right).

THE CONVENT COMPLEX

The basilica is part of a wider convent complex. The adjoining Capilla del Cristo de los Dolores is named after the image it contains – the *Christ of Sorrows* (1664), designed by Sebastián de Herrera. It depicts Christ with holes in His hands from the nails on the cross. To the south lies Dalieda de San Francisco, a peaceful garden with grand views over La Latina and the Casa de Campo.

9 The Wall Paintings

Five wall paintings **(above)** dominate the area behind the main chapel's High Altar, separated by gilt-trimmed columns. They depict scenes from the life of St Francis of Assisi.

10 The Sacristy

The basilica's sacristy is reached through the galleries and features beautifully carved wooden seats from the Renaissance. In the small chamber, one room further on, look out for Francisco Zurbarán's *San Bonaventure Visited by Thomas Aquinas* (1629).

🔟 ⭐ El Rastro

This vibrant street market, in one of the city's oldest working-class neighbourhoods, has been running since around 1840. The word *rastro* means "trail" and refers to the animal innards that were dragged through the streets when this was the site of the main abattoir. Goya immortalized the street types here in paintings such as *The Blind Guitarist*, while earlier the area had been the backdrop to satires by early 16th- to late 17th-century playwrights. Among the inhabitants were the Amazonas, a team of horsewomen who performed at royal receptions in the 16th century, and are remembered in Calle Amazonas.

Calle de la Ribera de Curtidores ①

The Rastro's main street is named after the *curtidores* (tanners) who once plied their trade here. You can still pick up a leather jacket at one of the dozens of stalls (right), as well as T-shirts, belts, handbags and hats.

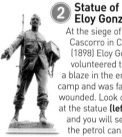

② Statue of Eloy Gonzalo

At the siege of Cascorro in Cuba (1898) Eloy Gonzalo volunteered to start a blaze in the enemy camp and was fatally wounded. Look closely at the statue (left) and you will see the petrol can.

③ Plaza del General Vara de Rey

Second-hand clothes, candelabras, books and old furniture are on offer in this bustling square.

④ Galerías Piquer

This famous shopping arcade surrounding a courtyard is named after the Valencian singer Concha Piquer. With around 70 shops selling beautiful furniture and decorative objects, it is a haven for antique enthusiasts.

Calle Carlos Arniches ⑤

Dropping away from the main square, this stall-lined street (right) marks the beginning of the flea market proper. The lock vendor is a regular fixture.

⑥ Calle Mira el Sol

The place to head to if you're after something electrical, including spare parts and mobile phones. The corner with Ribera de Curtidores is the favourite pitch of the *organillera* (female organ grinder).

⑨ Eating in El Rastro

There are many bars and cafés in the area. Malacatín **(below)**, at Calle de la Ruda 5, rustles up the delicious, meaty local stew *cocido Madrileño*.

⑦ Plaza Campillo del Mundo Nuevo

Collectors young and old browse the stacks of comics and magazines in the vicinity of this square **(above)**. You'll also find CDs, vinyl records, toys and oddities such as binoculars and magnifying glasses.

RÍO MANZANARES

The streets of the Rastro lead down to one of Madrid's most neglected features. The Manzanares River is famous only for being short on water and has been the butt of jokes since time immemorial. Until late in the 19th century, its banks were the haunt of *lavanderas* (washer-women), colourful figures who appear in the paintings of Francisco Goya. The Baroque bridge dates from 1719–32 and the sculptures of Madrid's patron saint, San Isidro are in the middle of it.

⑧ Stalls off Ribera de Curtidores

Painting equipment and picture frames are the speciality of Calle San Cayetano, while stalls near the Army & Navy store on Calle Carnero sell a wide range of sports gear. Pet owners should head for Calle Fray Ceferino González for the miscellany of dog collars, fishing nets and bird cages. There are also antique and furniture restoration shops.

⑩ Puerta de Toledo

This triumphal arch **(left)** was unveiled in 1827 and dedicated to Fernando VII. It was first proposed during the French occupation to extol the values of liberty and democracy.

NEED TO KNOW

MAP C5 ■ **Open** 9am–3pm Sun & public hols

■ Though the market traditionally sold only used goods, new items are now also sold.

■ The Rastro is rife with thieves and pickpockets. Keep a close eye on your valuables at all times.

TOP 10 ⭐ Museo Nacional Thyssen-Bornemisza

One of the most important art collections in the world focuses on European painting from the 13th to the 20th centuries. The wealthy industrialist Baron Heinrich Thyssen-Bornemisza began acquiring Old Masters in the 1920s for his villa in Switzerland. After the baron's death in 1947, his son, Hans Heinrich, added modern masterpieces, including French Impressionists, German Expressionists and the pick of the Russian Avant-Garde to the collection. In 1993, the state bought the 1,000-strong collection for the knock-down price of $350 million (the true value being estimated at nearly $1 billion). In 2005, an extension opened, displaying magnificent Impressionist works.

① Christ and the Samaritan Woman

Outstanding among the collection of Italian Primitives is this work (1310–11) by Sienese master Duccio di Buoninsegna (c.1255–1319). The painting's life-like quality **(right)** reveals Duccio's interest in accuracy, and anticipates the Renaissance.

② Rembrandt's Self-Portrait

This self-portrait (c.1643) by Rembrandt (1606–69) is one of more than 60 such works by the great Dutch artist. It reveals Rembrandt's view of himself as an isolated genius.

③ Young Knight in a Landscape

Vittore Carpaccio (c.1465–1525) is an important representative of the Venetian school. This intriguing work (1510) shows a courtly knight amid symbolic animals and plants **(below)**.

④ View of Alkmaar from the Sea

Dutch artist Salomon van Ruysdael's (1600–70) evocative seascape (c.1650) is considered to be one of the finest examples of the genre, for its effortless mastery of colour and carefully measured perspective.

⑤ Madonna of the Dry Tree

This devotional painting (c.1450) by Dutch artist Petrus Christus (c.1410–75) was inspired by an Old Testament metaphor in which God brings the dry tree (the chosen people) to life. The "A"s hanging from the tree stand for Ave Maria.

Key to Floorplan
First floor
Second floor

Museum Floorplan

9 Portrait of Henry VIII of England

During the 16th century, portraiture was a leading genre. When Hans Holbein, the Younger (c.1497–1543) was in the service of Henry VIII, he depicted the king (c.1537) in an almost frontal pose **(left)**. Henry's rich attire suggests that this was for a private room in Whitehall Palace.

6 Expulsion, Moon and Firelight

This haunting work (c.1828) is by Thomas Cole, American artist and founder of the Hudson River School. Cole idealized the untrammelled American landscape as a new Garden of Eden.

7 Still Life with Cat and Rayfish

This witty still life (c.1728) in the Dutch style is by the French artist, Jean-Baptiste-Siméon Chardin (1699–1779). Its companion piece, *Still Life with Cat and Fish*, is in Room 28.

8 Portrait of Giovanna Tornabuoni

This sublime portrait (1489) by Florentine artist Domenico Ghirlandaio (1449–94), was the last Baron Thyssen's favourite. It was commissioned to celebrate the marriage of Giovanna degli Albizzi to Lorenzo Tornabuoni – a union of two powerful families. Tragically, Giovanna died in childbirth shortly afterwards.

10 The Annunciation

Distorted figures, swirling lines and bold colours **(below)** are typical of the Mannerist style which El Greco (1541–1614) mastered in Venice, where he was influenced by Titian and Tintoretto. This intensely spiritual painting (c.1567–1577) reveals the Cretan artist's development following his move to Toledo, Spain, in 1577.

NEED TO KNOW

MAP F4 ■ Paseo del Prado 8 ■ 917 91 13 70 ■ www.museothyssen.org

Open 10am–7pm Tue–Sun (24 & 31 Dec: to 3pm); closed 1 Jan, 1 May & 25 Dec

Adm €13 (€9 concessions);

Permanent collection free noon–4pm Mon

■ The café-restaurant Las Terrazas has magnificent views of the garden.

■ The Thyssen opens for evening showings during summer, when you can enjoy a relaxed meal at the garden restaurant.

Museum Guide

The collection is organized chronologically, starting with Italian Primitives on the top floor and ending with 20th-century abstract and Pop Art. Temporary exhibitions are held on the ground floor and basement.

Modern Paintings in the Thyssen

Woman with a Parasol in a Garden by Renoir

1 Woman with a Parasol in a Garden

This painting (c.1873) is by one of the founders of the influential Impressionist movement, Pierre Auguste Renoir (1841–1919). Renoir was apprenticed for four years as a porcelain painter, and later attributed his technical brilliance in handling surface and texture to his early training.

2 Swaying Dancer

This exquisite study of a dancer in mid-performance (1877–9) by French artist Edgar Degas (1834–1917) is one of a series of his works devoted to the ballet. Unlike some of his fellow Impressionist painters, Degas placed great emphasis on the importance of drawing, as the superb draughtsmanship of this pastel clearly shows.

3 Les Vessenots

Vincent Van Gogh (1853–90) painted this dazzling rural landscape (1890) during the final year of his troubled life. He worked feverishly while staying at Les Vessenots, near Auvers in northern France, producing more than 80 canvases, mostly landscapes, (which were painted outdoors), in less than three months.

4 Fränzi in Front of a Carved Chair

Ernst Ludwig Kirchner (1880–1938) was an important figure in German Expressionism and a member of the group known as Die Brücke (The Bridge), which began the movement in Dresden. These artists were more interested in expressing feelings through their work, and encouraging emotional responses from their audience, rather than portraying outward reality. Fränzi Fehrmann, seen in this lovely work, dating from 1910, was one of their favourite models.

5 The Dream

A founder member, with Wassily Kandinsky, of the influential *Blaue Reiter* (Blue Rider) group, German artist Franz Marc (1880–1916) took Expressionism in a new, spiritual direction. Colours, as in this 1912 work, are used symbolically (blue was masculine and yellow feminine, for example), as are the animals in his paintings, which represent truth, beauty and other ideals.

6 Still Life with Instruments

One of the most creative artists Liubov Popova (1889–1924) was working in Russia in the period leading up to the

Swaying Dancer by Degas

Revolution. This Cubist painting (1915), completed after a period in Paris, is part of a suite of works called *Painterly Architectonics*, an even bolder example of which is exhibited in Room 41.

Modern Paintings Floorplan, Thyssen

Key to Floorplan
First floor

Still Life with Instruments by Popova

7 New York City
Piet Mondrian (1872–1944) was one of the most influential abstract artists of the 20th century. Born in the Netherlands, he moved to New York after the outbreak of World War II. The simple geometrical forms and bold colours of this abstract painting (1940–42) celebrate the energy and dynamism of his adopted home.

8 Brown and Silver I
Famous for his "action paintings" – random throwing or pouring of paint onto the canvas in an effort to create spontaneity – Jackson Pollock (1912–56) made a huge impact on postwar art in America. This painting (c.1951) is typical of the artist's revolutionary approach to making art.

9 Portrait of Baron H.H. Thyssen-Bornemisza
This revealing study of the museum's benefactor (1981–2) is the work of Britain's most distinguished portrait artist, Lucian Freud (1922–2011). In the background is *Pierrot Content* by Jean-Antoine Watteau (1684–1721), which visitors will find in Room 28.

10 Hotel Room
In this moving 1931 painting by American artist Edward Hopper (1882–1967), the bare furnishings, discarded suitcase and disconsolate posture of the woman holding the railway timetable masterfully suggest loneliness and dislocation – a subject the artist returned to repeatedly. Hopper is the most important representative of the American social realist school, created in the wake of the Wall Street Crash of 1929, and the Great Depression that followed.

Hotel Room by Edward Hopper

TOP 10 ⭐ Museo Nacional Centro de Arte Reina Sofía

The Reina Sofía's collection of 20th- and 21st-century Spanish art is exciting and challenging. The museum was inaugurated by King Juan Carlos and Queen Sofía in 1992. Besides the permanent collection, it also stages temporary exhibitions. There are works by the great masters of the interwar period – Juan Gris, Joan Miró, Salvador Dalí and Pablo Picasso, whose *Guernica* is the centrepiece of the gallery – and lesser-known artists are also featured.

1 Woman in Blue
This marvellous Blue-period portrait (1901) of an insolent-looking courtesan by Pablo Picasso (1881–1973) was painted from memory soon after his first visit to Paris. When it failed to win a national competition, a disgruntled Picasso discarded it.

2 Shout No. 7
Antonio Saura (1930–98) portrays the devastation after the Spanish Civil War in this painting (1959). He was a key exponent of the Spanish *art brut* trend which achieved international success in the late 1950s, once the Spanish borders were opened to artists.

3 Portrait of Sonia de Klamery (lying)
Hermenegildo Anglada-Camarasa (1871–1959) had a sensual style as this evocative painting (c.1913) shows.

4 The Gathering at the Café de Pombo
José Gutiérrez Solana (1886–1945) loved to record the social life of Madrid, as seen in this 1920 portrait **(below)**. The painting's owner, Ramón Gómez de la Serna, is shown in the centre.

Exterior of the Reina Sofía

5 Lying Figure
This nude by Francis Bacon (1909–92) was based on photographs of Henrietta Moraes by John Deakin, and depicts the distortion of the human form.

6 The Great Masturbator
Catalan artist Salvador Dalí (1904–89) was a leading exponent of Surrealism, with its exploration of the subconscious. The figure of the *Masturbator* (1929) is derived from a weird rock formation at Cadaqués, close to where Dalí had a home.

Accidente ⑦

Also known as *Self-portrait*, Alfonso Ponce de León's (1906–36) disturbing work **(right)** was painted during the last year of his life, and prefigures his tragic execution during the Spanish Civil War. The painting, which shows a man violently thrown from a vehicle, is a mixture of realistic elements, along with lack of depth, flat colour and artificial lighting, which reflect the artist's use of both Surrealism and Magic Realism.

Portrait II ⑧

Joan Miró (1893–1983) encompassed Cubism and Surrealism but he never lost his extraordinary originality. In this 1938 work **(right)** the Catalan painter is more interested in juxtaposing colours rather than revealing the physical attributes of the sitter.

Superimposition of Grey Matter ⑨

Antoni Tàpies's (1923–2012) "matter paintings" explore texture and are composed by adding layers of mixed media, such as sand, powdered marble and paint, onto a pre-varnished canvas.

Open Window ⑩

Juan Gris (1887–1927) became one of Cubism's leading exponents. This 1921 work is an excellent example.

NEED TO KNOW

MAP F6 ■ Calle Santa Isabel 52 ■ 917 74 10 00 ■ www.museoreinasofia.es

Open 10am–9pm Wed–Mon; closed Tue, 1 & 6 Jan, 1 & 15 May, 9 Nov, 24, 25 Dec & 31 Dec

Adm €12 (free 7–9pm Mon–Sat, 12:30–2:30pm Sun)

■ **NuBel café-restaurant on the ground floor of the Nouvel Building has** a daily set-price menu and is accessed from the museum, or from Calle Argumosa 43.

■ **The museum shop sells Spanish designer jewellery, ceramics, books, slides and posters.**

Museum Guide

The entrance to the main Sabatini Building is in Plaza Juan Goytisolo. Permanent collections can be found on the first, second and fourth floors, and temporary exhibitions on the first and third floors. Further permanent collections are in the Nouvel Building. Exhibits are susceptible to change. Throughout 2021, the museum is opening new exhibition spaces on the ground floor, which will house artworks from the 1990s to the present day, including a section devoted to architecture.

Sculptures in the Reina Sofía

 1 Tetapop
Ángela García Codoñer (València, 1944) finds inspiration in the aesthetics of Pop Art, and this work (1973) playfully alludes to the feminist gaze in Spanish sculpure.

Key to Floorplan

☐ First floor
☐ Second floor
☐ Fourth floor

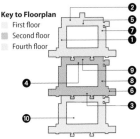

Sculptures in the Reina Sofía

2 Spider
Louise Bourgeois (1911–2010) used spiders as the subject of a number of drawings and sculptures throughout her varied career. She created this one, first exhibited in 1994, to ambiguously allude to the role of the mother.

 3 Sick Child
Medardo Rosso (1858–1928) prefigured aspects of modern sculpture with this striking bust of a suffering child (1895), which he hoped would capture the psychological nuance and complexity of his subject.

4 Dancer
With this remarkably energetic sculpture (1989), avant-garde Spanish artist Alberto Sánchez uses cement and wood to channel the dynamic energy of the dancer.

5 Bicho Maquina (Creature Machine)
Brazilian artist Lygia Clark (1920–88) designed this aluminium, geometric sculpture (1962) to be mobile, playing with our ideas of permanence by making a piece that can be endlessly reworked.

Sánchez's _Dancer_

6 Sailor with Guitar
Born in Lithuania, Jacques Lipchitz (1891–1973) fell under the spell of Cubism during his first stay in Paris in 1909. This piece (1917) is one of his several Cubist sculptures.

7 Empty Suspension
Jorge de Oteiza (1908–2003) was a highly original Basque sculptor. This forged steel sculpture (1957) was developed around the time the artist was taking an interest in American megalithic statuary.

8 Bather
Spanish sculptor Mateo Hernández (1884–1949) produced work influenced by Art Deco and New Objectivity trends during the interwar years. _Bather_ (1925) follows the Ancient Greek style of being carved in coral granite.

9 Woman in the Garden
In the late 1920s, Picasso frequented the studio of Catalan artist Julio González in Paris, and was inspired to develop his own metal sculpting techniques. Results include this remark-able bronze _Woman in the Garden_ (1930–32).

10 Toki Egin (Homage to St John of the Cross)
Eduardo Chillida (1924–2002) is one of Spain's most highly regarded sculptors. This huge iron work (1989–90) weighs 9,000 kg (17,500 lbs) – cranes were used to install it in the garden.

PABLO PICASSO'S GUERNICA

Spanish town of Guernica, after the bombing by German and Italian aircraft in 1937

TOP 10
FEATURES IN PICASSO'S GUERNICA

1 Bull
2 Wounded Horse
3 Bereaved Mother
4 Dead Child
5 Dead Soldier
6 Candle
7 Light Bulb
8 Broken Dagger
9 Window
10 Eyes

The museum's most precious and famous work is on display in Room 206. Commissioned as propaganda, *Guernica* instantly transcended its original purpose. In April 1937, at the height of the Civil War, German bombers devastated the Basque town of Guernica (Gernika) in support of General Franco's Nationalist forces. The attack, almost unprecedented, on a defenceless civilian population, caused international outrage. Picasso completed his huge canvas in just two months and it was first exhibited at the Paris World's Fair. Ever since, the meaning and content of *Guernica* have been minutely analysed, to the irritation of the artist. Picasso chose not to depict the bombardment – there are no airplanes, for example – but to indict war, with all its senselessness and barbarity, conceived in terms of the artist's highly individual language of symbols. The preliminary sketches (some of which are on display in the adjacent rooms) help the viewer to understand the work. Picasso tried eight different versions before arriving at his ultimate vision.

Guernica's **symbolism** of dismembered bodies, staring eyes, rearing horses gripped in pain, and desperate outstretched arms, combined with the bleakness of a mono-chrome colour scheme, express the artist's view of war.

TOP 10 ★ Parque del Retiro

The Retiro is the city's green lung and the *Madrileños'* favourite weekend retreat. The aristocracy was admitted to the former royal grounds in 1767 but it was another century before the gates were opened to the general public. Visitors can enjoy the park's decorative features, which include statues, follies, a formal French garden and a boating lake, as well as the numerous amenities. Children will make a beeline for the puppet theatre, while adults may prefer the concerts at the bandstand. Sunday, when there is almost a carnival atmosphere, is the best day to enjoy everything from circus acts and buskers to pavement artists and fortune-tellers.

Estanque ①

The boating lake **(right)** is one of the oldest features of the park (1631). In the days of Felipe IV, it was the setting for mock naval battles. Rowing boats are available for hire from the jetty. Once in a while the lake is drained for cleaning and 6,000 fish have to find a temporary home.

② Puerta de la Independencia

The handsome Independence Gate **(below)** does not rightfully belong here. It was designed by Antonio López

Aguado as the entrance to a palace built by Fernando VII for his second wife, Isabel de Bragança. It is, however, the most important of the 18 gates.

Monument to Alfonso XII ③

This huge monument **(below)** was conceived in 1898 as a defiant response to Spain's humiliating defeat in Cuba, but the plans were not realised until 1922. The equestrian statue of the king is by Mariano Benlliure. The most impressive feature is the handsome curved colonnade, lined with bronze sculptures. It is a popular spot with sun-worshippers.

Plan of the Parque del Retiro

④ Palacio de Velázquez

The Retiro's exhibition centre is the work of Ricardo Velázquez Bosco. The tiled frieze perfectly offsets the pink and yellow brick banding **(above)**.

⑤ Paseo de las Estatuas

This line of Baroque statues, representing the kings and queens of Spain, was intended to impress other Iberian rulers and the Aztec chief Montezuma.

⑥ Rosaleda

The rose garden **(above)** holds more than 4,000 roses of 100 different varieties. Designed in 1915 by the city's head gardener, Cecilio Rodríguez, it is modelled on the Bagatelle in the Bois de Boulogne, Paris.

NEED TO KNOW

MAP G4 ■ Puerta de Alcalá
■ 915 30 00 41

Open Apr–Sep: 6am–midnight (Oct–Mar: to 10pm daily)

■ Refreshment kiosks can be found at various points in the park.

■ In June a major book fair takes place, popular with parents and children.

---

⑦ Casita del Pescador

The "fisherman's house", a typical *capricho* (whim) of the era, was a part of the re-landscaping of the park in the 1820s. A water-wheel, concealed by the grotto and artificial hill, creates a cascade.

⑧ Fuente de la Alcachofa

The "artichoke fountain" was designed by Ventura Rodríguez, and made of Sierra de Guadarrama granite and Colmenar stone. The artichoke at the top is supported by four cherubs.

⑨ El Ángel Caído

This beguiling sculpture **(right)**, the work of Ricardo Bellver, is said to be the only public monument to the "fallen angel" (Lucifer) in the world. It was unveiled in 1878.

⑩ Palacio de Cristal

Mirrored in a lake and framed by trees, the Crystal Palace *(see p73)* was inspired by its British namesake in 1887.

THE BUEN RETIRO PALACE

The park's full title, Parque del Buen Retiro, is a reference to the palace built for Felipe IV in 1630–32 near the Jerónimos Monastery – *retiro* means retreat. It was vandalized by French troops during the War of Independence, and eventually demolished. The only parts to survive – the ballroom and the Salón de Reinos – have been earmarked as annexes of the Prado *(see pp16–21)*.

🔟 ⭐ Museo Arqueológico Nacional

The National Archaeology Museum of Spain occupies an impressive Neo-Classical building in the elegant Salamanca neighbourhood, and contains more than 1,300,000 artworks and artifacts that span millennia, and have been gathered from around the world. After an expensive and lengthy renovation, the museum reopened its doors in 2014 with more than 10,000 sq m (12,000 sq yds) of gallery space to show off its dazzling collection. Major attractions include enigmatic female statues, sculpted by Iberian tribes more than 2,000 years ago, glittering collections of Visigothic goldwork and even some curious and unique early calculators.

Tesoro de Guarrazar ①

This magnificent hoard of Visigothic votive crowns and crosses, discovered in a Spanish orchard in the mid-19th century, dates back to the 7th century. One of the finest pieces is the golden votive Crown of Recesvinto, studded with blue sapphires **(right)**.

② Dama de Elche

This is Spain's answer to the *Mona Lisa* **(left)** – a polychrome bust of a female figure which dates from the 4th century BC. The *Lady of Elche* is remarkable for its sophistication, the superb quality of the carving and the woman's enigmatic expression.

③ Coin and Medal Collection

The museum's collection of coins and medals is one of the largest and finest in Europe. Among the earliest coins are a Carthaginian trishekel and a silver tetradrachm engraved with the profile of Ptolemy IV, both of which date to the 3rd century BC.

Bote de Zamora ④

This exquisitely carved, ivory urn **(right)** is considered to be one of the greatest jewels of Islamic art, and was commissioned by Al-Hakam II, the Caliph of Cordoba, for Subh, a Basque slave who became his favourite concubine but died young.

⑤ Dama de Baza

A remarkable Iberian statue depicting a female figure, the 4th-century BC Lady of Baza is seated on an armchair **(left)**, and features the same inscrutable expression as her more celebrated neighbour in the same gallery.

⑥ Estela de Solana de Cabañas

Dating back to between 1000 and 800 BC, this Bronze Age engraved stone discovered in Cáceres is thought to be a funerary stela, and depicts a heroic figure surrounded by chariots and weapons **(right)**.

⑦ Puteal de la Moncloa

This large Roman marble well is carved with graceful figures from Greek myths, including the birth of Athena in Olympus. The well was acquired by Felipe V in the 18th century.

⑧ Orante Sumerio

Purchased for the museum's collection in 2007, this elegant praying figure was carved around 2,500 BC in Mesopotamia (now Iraq). Sumerian votive figures like this one were commissioned for temples.

⑨ Husillos Sarcophagus

The museum has an extensive collection of Roman art and statuary. This decorated sarcophagus **(below)**, carved in Rome for a wealthy patron and brought to Hispania, depicts the story of Orestes, who figures prominently in several Greek tragedies.

⑩ Ábaco Neperiano

This cabinet of bronze and ivory rods and strips, engraved with multiplication tables **(left)**, is a rare 17th-century calculator. It was invented by John Napier of Edinburgh and is often called "Napier's bones".

NEED TO KNOW

MAP X9 ■ Calle Serrano, 13 ■ 915 77 79 12 ■ www.man.mcu.es

Open 9:30am–8pm Tue–Sat (to 3pm Sun & public hols); closed 1 & 6 Jan, 1 May, 9 Nov and 24, 25 & 31 Dec

Adm €3 (free 2–8pm Sat, 9:30am–3pm Sun)

■ It has a shop and a café with a terrace.

■ A free multimedia app featuring an interactive guide (also suitable for the sight- and hearing-impaired) is available – search for MAN Museo Arqueológico Nacional on your device.

Museum Guide
The main entrance is on Calle Serrano. The collection is laid out chronologically, with the Prehistoric section on the ground floor; Roman, Late Antiquity, Medieval Al-Andalus and Protohistory galleries on the first floor, and the Modern and Medieval Era collections on the second floor. Coins and medals are displayed on a mezzanine level between the first and second floors. The museum's star exhibit, Dama de Elche is found in Room 13.

🔟 ⭐ El Escorial

Occupying a majestic setting in the southern foothills of the Sierra de Guadarrama, the Royal Monastery of San Lorenzo de El Escorial was commissioned by Felipe II as a mausoleum for the tomb of his father, Carlos I. The name commemorates the victory over the French at St Quentin on the Feast of St Lawrence in 1557. Building began in 1563 and the king took a keen interest in the smallest details. The complex was completed in 1595 and comprised a basilica, a royal palace, a monastery, a seminary and a library. This monument to the king's personal aspirations, and the ideals of the Counter-Reformation still inspires awe, if not always affection, and is a UNESCO World Heritage Site.

1 Basilica

The basilica (below) takes the form of a Greek cross, and has vaults decorated with exquisite frescoes by Luca Giordano.

Sierra de Guadarrama and Monasterio de El Escorial

3 Pantheon of the Kings

Work on the domed burial chamber, situated directly under the high altar of the basilica, was completed in 1654. The walls were surfaced with marble, bronze and jasper by Giovanni Battista Crescenzi.

4 Library

The magnificent barrel-vaulted hall (below) has stunning ceiling frescoes by Italian artists. The shelves contain 4,000 precious manuscripts and 40,000 folio volumes that are arranged facing outwards to allow air to permeate the pages.

2 King's Apartments

King Felipe II's personal quarters are surprisingly modest – just three simply furnished rooms with white-washed walls and terracotta tiling. Look out for the hand chair that was used to carry the gout-ridden king on his last journey here in 1598.

FELIPE II'S VISION

Before architect Juan Bautista de Toledo could start on El Escorial, Felipe II gave him precise instructions: "[It should have] simplicity in the construction, severity in the whole, nobility without arrogance, majesty without ostentation." It was designed to resemble the iron grid on which St Lawrence was burned.

5 Main Staircase

Look upwards from this magnificent staircase to admire the "Glory of the Spanish monarchy" frescoes **(above)** by Luca Giordano.

7 Strolling Gallery

Felipe II enjoyed indoor walks in this airy gallery. The meridians on the floor were added in the 18th century.

8 Courtyard of the Kings

This courtyard **(below)** offers the best view of the basilica façade, its twin belltowers and awe-inspiring dome. Look out for the larger-than-life statues over the portal, of Old Testament kings.

6 Gallery of Battles

This gallery is decorated with superb frescoes by 16th-century Italian artists. The paintings were intended to validate Felipe II's military campaigns.

9 Chapter Houses

The vaulted ceilings were decorated in the 17th century by Italian artists Fabrizio Castello and Nicolas Granelo. Hanging from the walls are priceless canvases by Titian, Tintoretto, Veronese, Velázquez and El Greco.

10 Architecture Museum

This small exhibition of plans, scale models and workmen's tools explains how El Escorial was constructed. Note the wooden cranes and hoists used to haul the blocks of granite into place.

NEED TO KNOW

MAP A1 ■ Calle de Juan de Borbón y Battenberg ■ 918 90 59 04 ■ www.patrimonionacional.es

Open Royal Monastery and Palace: Apr–Sep: 10am–7pm Tue–Sun (Oct–Mar: to 6pm); Gardens: Apr–Sep: 10am–8pm daily; closed 1 & 6 Jan, 1 May, 11 Sep, 24, 25 & 31 Dec

Adm €12, €6 (concessions), additional €4 for a guided tour, free 3pm–closing time Wed–Sun, 18 May & 12 Oct

■ The Bourbon rooms (Aposentos de los Borbones), Casa del Príncipe Don Carlos and Casa del Infante Don Gabriel can only be visited as part of the guided tour.

■ Train C-8 from Atocha-Cercanías station to El Escorial; bus to San Lorenzo de El Escorial; buses 661 & 664 from Moncloa to San Lorenzo El Escorial.

■ It can get very cold inside the monastery in winter so dress warmly.

Further Features of El Escorial

1 Cenotaphs

These superb bronze sculptures on either side of the high altar are by an Italian father and son team – Leone and Pompeo Leoni. On the left is Carlos I (Emperor Charles V), shown with his wife, daughter and sisters; opposite are Felipe II, three of his wives and his son, Don Carlos.

Calvary by Rogier van der Weyden

2 King's Deathbed

In this simple canopied bed, Felipe II died on 13 September 1598, it is said as "the seminary children were singing the dawn mass". The bed was positioned so that the king could easily see the high altar of the basilica on one side and the mountains of the Sierra de Guadarrama on the other.

3 The Martyrdom of St Maurice and the Theban Legion

This ethereal work by El Greco (1541–1614) was intended for an altar in the basilica, but Felipe II found the style inappropriate and relegated it to the sacristy. El Greco never received another royal commission.

4 Portrait of Felipe II

In this stately painting by Dutch artist Antonio Moro, the king, then aged 37, is wearing the suit of armour he wore at the battle of St Quentin in France in 1557. It was to be Felipe's only victory on the battlefield.

5 Cellini Crucifix

Florentine master craftsman Benvenuto Cellini sculpted this exquisite image of Christ from a single block of Carrara marble. It was presented to Felipe II in 1562 by Francisco de Medici, Grand Duke of Tuscany.

6 Calvary

This moving painting is by 15th-century Flemish artist Rogier van der Weyden. Felipe II knew the Netherlands well and was an avid collector of Flemish art.

7 Last Supper

Venetian artist Titian undertook numerous commissions for El Escorial. Unfortunately his *Last Supper* canvas was too big to fit the space assigned to it in the monks' refectory and was literally cut down to size.

8 Inlay Doors

One of the most striking features of the king's apartments is the superb marquetry of the inlay doors. Made by German craftsmen in the 16th century, they were sent as a gift to Felipe II from Emperor Maximilian II.

9 King's Treasures

A cupboard in the royal bedchamber contains more than a dozen priceless *objets d'art*. They include a 12th-century chest made in Limoges and a 16th-century "peace plate" by Spanish craftsman Luís de Castillo.

10 Queen's Room Organ

The corridors of El Escorial would have resounded to monastic plainchant, but organ music also met with royal approval. This hand organ dates from the 16th century and is decorated with Felipe II's coat of arms.

KING FELIPE II

When Felipe II took over the reins of government from his father Carlos I in 1556, he inherited not only the Spanish kingdoms of Castile and Aragon, Naples, Sicily, Milan and the Low Countries, but also the Spanish territories of the New World. Defending this far-flung empire embroiled him in constant warfare. The drain on the royal coffers

Felipe II

(despite the prodigious influx of gold and silver from the Americas) led to unpopular tax increases at home, and eventual bankruptcy. Felipe's enemies, the Protestant Dutch, their English allies and the Huguenot French set out to blacken his reputation, portraying him as a cold and bloodthirsty tyrant. Today's historians take a more objective view, revealing him to have been a conscientious, if rather remote, ruler, and a model family man with a wry sense of humour. On one occasion he startled the monks of El Escorial by encouraging an Indian elephant to roam the cloisters and invade the monastic cells.

**TOP 10
EL ESCORIAL
STATISTICS**

1 2,673 windows
2 1,200 doors
3 300 monastic cells
4 88 fountains
5 86 stairways
6 73 statues
7 42 chapels (basilicas)
8 16 courtyards
9 14 entrance halls
10 500,000 visitors a year

A fine illustration of the Monastery of El Escorial dating from the 16th century, Biblioteca Nacional.

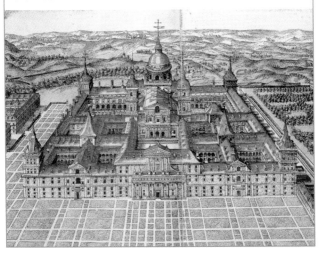

The Top 10 of Everything

Traditional Iberian tin-glazed
ceramic tiles, known as *azulejos*

🔟 Moments in History

Auto-da-fé in the Plaza Mayor (1680) by Francisco Rizi, Prado Museum

1 Birth of a City

The first inhabitants of Madrid were Muslim soldiers under the command of Muhammad I. The founding of the city is usually dated to AD 852 when a fortress *(alcázar)* was built on the escarpment now occupied by the Palacio Real *(see pp12–15)*. Few traces of this early settlement survive, apart from a small section of the city walls, the Muralla Árabe defences *(see p112)*.

2 Christian Conquest

Muhammad I had his fortress built to guard against attack from northern Christian armies, and to protect the important city of Toledo. In 1083 Toledo fell and the *Alcázar* of Madrid was surrendered without a fight. The new Christian settlers lived harmoniously with their Arab neighbours, but mosques were changed to churches.

3 New Capital

In 1561 Felipe II took the decision to make Madrid his new capital (previously Valladolid was the preferred city). The central location and proximity to other royal residences were determining factors.

Felipe II

Madrid was still a small, squalid town of 9,000 inhabitants – one of the king's first decisions was to transform the old marketplace outside the walls into a public square, now Plaza Mayor *(see pp22–3)*.

4 Flourishing of the Spanish Arts

By the time that Plaza Mayor was completed in 1619, Madrid's population had swollen to around 85,000. Courtiers, noblemen, clerics and criminals descended on the city, leading to such overcrowding that Felipe IV ordered a new perimeter wall to be built. Madrid provided rich material for playwrights, including Lope de Vega and Tirso de Molina.

5 Mayor-King

Madrid thrived during the reign of Carlos III (1759–88). He gave the city magnificent gateways such as the Puerta de Alcalá *(see p82)*, and imposing thoroughfares such as the Paseo del Prado *(see pp78–83)*. Streets were paved and lit, sewers were dug and nightwatchmen introduced. He became known as *El Rey-Alcalde* (the Mayor-King).

6 Insurrection
On 2 May 1808, two months after a French army occupied the city, the people of Madrid rose in revolt. Fierce street battles were fought, while the troops of the Monteleón barracks mutinied in support of the rebels. But within a few hours, the insurrection had been crushed and the leaders were executed by firing squad.

7 Re-Awakening
In 1919 Alfonso XIII opened Madrid's first metro line and the city was – literally – on the move again, after decades of inertia. Whole streets were demolished to make way for the Gran Vía's bars and restaurants, and Calle de Alcalá became the heart of a new financial district.

8 Madrid Under Siege
Three months into the Spanish Civil War, General Franco's Nationalist army surrounded Madrid. Republican resistance was fierce and the siege dragged on for two-and-a-half years, with the city eventually falling to the rebel forces in March 1939.

9 Death of Franco

After ruling Spain with an iron fist for 36 years, General Franco died in November 1975, leaving power in the hands of his designated successor, Prince (later King) Juan Carlos I. The first democratic elections were held in June 1977.

General Franco

10 Tejero's Coup
On 23 February 1981, Franco loyalists under Colonel Antonio Tejero attempted a coup. Tejero forced his way into the parliament building, firing shots into the air. The conspiracy collapsed when the king confirmed that the army had remained loyal.

TOP 10 FIGURES IN MADRID'S HISTORY

1 Al-Mundhir
According to some historians, Muhammad I's son was the true founder of the city.

2 Isidro Merlo y Quintana
This devout farm labourer inspired miracles after his death in 1172 and became the city's patron saint.

3 Felipe II
When in Madrid, the king stayed in the Alcázar or with the monks of San Jerónimo Monastery.

4 Félix Lope de Vega
This leading Spanish playwright was banned from Madrid for eight years after libelling his former lover's father.

5 Carlos III
Although Madrid's "best mayor" spent little of the first part of his reign in the city, his long-term impact is undeniable.

6 Manuela Malasaña
A brave heroine, Malasaña died fighting against Joseph Bonaparte's troops during the insurrection in May 1808.

7 Joseph Bonaparte
Although detested during his short reign as King of Spain (1808–13), he did plan one of the city's finest squares, Plaza de Oriente *(see p103)*.

8 Gustavo Durán
One of the most courageous commanders who defended Madrid during the Civil War.

9 Clara Campoamor
The first woman to defend women's right to vote, Campoamor paved the way for female suffrage in 1931.

10 Enrique Tierno Galván
A popular mayor, who ran the city from 1979 until his death in 1986, during a time of great cultural change.

Enrique Tierno Galván

🔟 Museums and Galleries

Beautifully ornate Salón Chaflán at the Museo Cerralbo

1 Museo Cerralbo

This astonishingly diverse collection – paintings, sculptures, tapestries, glassware, porcelain and more – was originally the property of the 17th Marquis of Cerralbo. The museum's (see p101) 30,000 artifacts are housed in his palace and the rooms offer a fascinating window onto the life of Spanish aristocracy at the beginning of the 20th century.

2 Museo Nacional del Prado

The famous gallery (see pp16–21) is housed in Juan de Villanueva's Neo-Classical masterpiece – an artistic monument in its own right. The relief above the Velázquez Portal depicts Fernando VII as guardian of the arts and sciences – it was during his reign that the Prado opened as an art gallery. Its strongest collection, unsurprisingly, is its Spanish artworks, particularly those of Goya.

3 Museo Nacional Thyssen-Bornemisza

The setting for this outstanding collection is the Palacio de Villahermosa,

remodelled in the 1990s and with a dramatic new wing added in 2005. Carmen Thyssen-Bornemisza, widow of the preceding baron, was responsible for the salmon-pink colour scheme inside. The museum (see pp28–31) holds international art from the 14th century onwards.

4 Museo Nacional Centro de Arte Reina Sofía

This treasure-house (see pp32–5) of modern Spanish art was designed as a hospital by Francisco Sabatini in 1756. The conversion to art gallery was completed in 1990. The glass lifts offer panoramic views of the city.

5 Museo de América

While the fabled treasures shipped back to Spain by Cortés, Columbus and Pizarro were exhibited as early as 1519, most of the precious items disappeared or were melted down. A great many of the ethnological and ethnographical exhibits on show here (see p101) originate from Carlos III's "cabinet of natural history", founded in the 18th century, and the museum's displays now embrace the entire American continent.

Quimbaya gold censer, Museo de América

⑥ Museo Arqueológico Nacional

Founded by Queen Isabel II in 1867, the archaeological museum *(see pp38–9)* contains treasures from most of the world's ancient civilizations, with an emphasis on the Iberian Peninsula. Highlights includes "Lady of Elche", the carved sculpture of a noblewoman from the 4th century BC.

⑦ Real Academia de Bellas Artes de San Fernando

The Academy of Fine Arts *(see p94)* was founded by Fernando VI in 1752 and moved into the Goyeneche Palace 25 years later. Among the highlights are works by Spanish artists El Greco, Velázquez, Murillo, Zurbarán and Goya, as well as an array of European masterpieces.

⑧ Casa-Museo de Lope de Vega

Spain's greatest playwright Félix Lope de Vega *(see p47)* lived in this house between 1610 and 1635. Now a museum *(see p108)*, its rooms are furnished in the style of the period, based on an inventory by the dramatist himself.

⑨ Museo Sorolla

The home of Valencian artist Joaquín Sorolla (1863–1923) is now a museum *(see p87)* displaying his work. Sorolla won international recognition after his paintings were shown in the Exposition Universelle in Paris (1901). His canvases are evocations of Spanish life. One of his best-loved works depicts his wife and daughter on Valencia's seashore.

Walk on the Beach **by Sorolla at Museo Sorolla**

⑩ Museo Nacional de Artes Decorativas

One of the many highlights of the Decorative Arts Museum *(see p81)* is that it sets Spanish crafts in a European context. Highlights include a Gothic bedroom, Flemish tapestries and a lovely collection of 19th-century fans.

🔟 Architectural Sights

Baroque-style ceiling of Palacio Real

1 Palacio Real

The stunning Royal Palace (see pp12–15) marks a decisive break with the austere tastes of Spain's Habsburg rulers. Felipe V had been brought up at Versailles where the International Baroque style was in vogue. Architect Filippo Juvarra died two years into the project, but his successor, Giovanni Battista Sacchetti retained the Baroque spirit.

2 Plaza Mayor

The inspiration for the square (see pp22–3) was El Escorial's courtyard (see pp40–43). But the plans of architect Juan de Herrera were realized only 30 years later, in 1619, by Gómez de Mora.

3 Palacio de Cibeles

MAP F4 ■ Plaza Cibeles 1

Home of the Madrid Town Hall since 2007, this extraordinary building was the first major commission of Galician architect Antonio Palacios and his partner, Joaquín Otamendi. The style of this palace (1907–19) has influences ranging from Spanish Plateresque to Art Nouveau. The most striking feature of the interior is the glass-domed roof.

4 Palacio Longoria

Art Nouveau is usually associated with Barcelona rather than with Madrid and, in fact, this superb example is by the Catalan architect José Grases Riera. Bold and original in design, the palace (see p120) is full of typical Art Nouveau features, such as the florid sculptural detail, sensuous curves and the balustrade.

5 Círculo de Bellas Artes

The Fine Arts Club (see p94) dates from the 1920s and is Antonio Palacios' Art Deco masterpiece. The crowning feature is the statue on the roof (see p59), representing the goddess Minerva, patroness of the arts. Pay the one-day membership fee and you can see the other highlights – the staircase, theatre, ballroom and the Salón de Fiestas, with its painted ceiling.

6 Edificio Metrópolis

One of Madrid's signature buildings, Edificio Metrópolis (see p94) was designed in 1905 by the French architects Jules and Raymond Février. The high points of this lovely Neo-Baroque design are the bronze wreaths garlanding the cupola, which glint in the sunlight.

The striking Edificio Metrópolis

7 Parroquia de San Jerónimo el Real

Though much altered over the years, this 16th-century parish church (see p82) is an important architectural monument. It has also served as a refuge for Spanish kings and queens through the ages. Former king Juan Carlos I was crowned here in 1975 after the death of General Franco.

8 Puerta de Europa

Plaza de Castilla ▪ Metro Plaza de Castilla

The "Gateway to Europe" is a modern version of a triumphal arch. Twenty-six storeys high, these imposing, leaning towers of glass and metal were completed in 1996.

The majestic Puerta de Europa

9 Residencia de Estudiantes

Pabellón Transatlántico, Calle del Pinar 21 ▪ Metro Pinar del Rey ▪ Guided tours: 11am–8pm Mon–Sat (to 3pm Sun); email visita@residencia. csic.es to book

Salvador Dalí and Federico García Lorca attended this college founded in 1910. Designed by Antonio Flórez, the main building was nicknamed "transatlantic" as the balustrade resembled the rail of an ocean liner.

10 Torre de Cristal

Paseo de la Castellana 259 ▪ Metro Begoña ▪ Closed to the public

This is Spain's tallest skyscraper at 249 m (817 ft). It was designed by Argentinian architect César Pelli, who also laid out Brookfield Place in New York City. Occupying the upper floors is a vertical garden designed by French botanist Patrick Blanc.

TOP 10 PLACES TO SEE AZULEJOS (TILES)

Entrance to Fatigas del Querer

1 Fatigas del Querer
The interior of this 1920's tavern (see p98) is decorated with Andalucían tiles and murals.

2 Taberna la Dolores
MAP E5 ▪ Plaza Jesús 4
Tiled mosaics adorn the façade of this taberna dating from 1908.

3 Viva Madrid, Taberna Inusual
Tiled inside and out; look for the Cibeles fountain on the façade (see p115).

4 Tablao Flamenco 1911
Fantastic ceramic decor dates from the days when this restaurant (see p115) became a flamenco club.

5 El Doble
MAP R2 ▪ Calle de Ponzano 58
Covered in beautiful decorative tiles inside and out, this is one of the best breweries in Madrid and serves great draft beers.

6 Taberna Ángel Sierra
Stunning tiled façade and interior, from the early 20th century (see p125).

7 Taberna Almendro 13
Andalucían decor can be found in this typical tapas bar (see p116).

8 La Fontana de Oro
MAP P4 ▪ Calle de la Victoria 1
Pretty, historic café converted into a Guinness pub.

9 Taberna Tirso de Molina
MAP N6 ▪ Plaza de Tirso Molina 9
The façade here features modern tiles reproducing works by French poster artist Toulouse-Lautrec.

10 Taberna de la Daniela
Ceramic motifs cover the bar and façade of this classic Madrid taberna (see p90).

TOP 10 Parks and Gardens

The Palacio de Cristal exhibition space in the Parque del Retiro

1 Parque del Retiro

In 1767, Carlos III broke with tradition by allowing members of the public into the Retiro *(see pp36–7)*, providing they were "washed and suitably dressed". However it was not until the 1860s and the advent of the First Republic that the partitions separating the royal enclosure from the public area were finally torn down for good.

2 Real Jardín Botánico

The botanical garden *(see pp80–81)* is the perfect place to recharge your batteries after the exhausting walk around the Prado Museum. The shady paths are lined with statues, and the air is cooled by judiciously placed fountains.

3 Jardines del Campo del Moro

MAP A4 ■ Open Apr–Sep: 10am–8pm daily; Oct–Mar: 10am–6pm daily ■ Closed for some official ceremonies, check website before visiting

Surprisingly, these gardens *(see p13)* in the grounds of the Palacio Real were not laid out until the 19th century. The name, "Moor's field" refers to the Arab general, Ali Ben Youssef, who is said

to have camped here while besieging the city after it had fallen to the Christians in 1109. On a fine day, the views of the palace and the Casa de Campo from these gardens are unbeatable. These beautiful gardens feature about 70 species of trees.

Fountain at Campo del Moro gardens

4 Parque del Oeste

MAP B2 ■ Paseo Moret ■ Closed to cars on weekends

This lovely park was designed in the early 20th century by Cecilio Rodríguez, head gardener at the Retiro *(see p61)*. Apart from the *rosaleda* (rose garden), the main attraction is the Temple of Debod, an ancient monument dating from the 2nd century BC. It was a gift from the Egyptian government. Cafés abound on Paseo del Pintor Rosales, which is also a terminus of the Teleférico cable car.

⑤ Casa de Campo
Paseo Puerta del Angel 1 (bicycles only) ▪ **Metro Lago or Casa de Campo**

The city's largest green space, and Felipe II's favourite hunting ground, was opened to the public with the overthrow of the monarchy in 1931. Attractively planted with pines, oaks, poplars and many other trees, there are also huge areas of open space, mostly scrub. Amenities include cafés, picnic areas, restaurants, a boating lake, a zoo and the lively Parque de Atracciones *(see p60)* amusement park.

⑥ Parque Juan Carlos I
Avenida de Logroño, 26 ▪ **Metro Feria de Madrid** ▪ **Open Jun–Sep: 7–1am daily; Oct–May: 7am–11pm Sun–Thu, 7am–midnight Fri & Sat**

This attractive park *(see p73)* lies within the exhibition grounds of the Campo de las Naciones. Highlights include catamaran trips on the river, superb modern sculptures and a train that runs through the park every half an hour.

⑦ Jardines de Sabatini
MAP J2 ▪ **Calle de Bailén, 2** ▪ **Open May–Sep: 9am–10pm daily; Oct–Apr: 9am–9pm daily**

These orderly gardens next to the Palacio Real are set in the royal stables. Although the gardens were laid out in the 1930s, the design was based on the original 18th-century plans. The gardens are ideal for a picnic and offer breathtaking sunset views.

⑧ Parque de Berlín
Avenida de Ramón y Cajal, 2 ▪ **Metro Concha Espina**

Set among the fountains at the far end of this park, near the Auditorio Nacional de Música *(see p63)*, are three sections of the Berlin Wall with original graffiti. Children's play areas and places to eat and drink are nearby.

⑨ Invernadero de Atocha
MAP F6 ▪ **Plaza Emperador Carlos V s/n** ▪ **Open daily**

The space beneath the iron-and-glass canopy at Madrid's central railway station is occupied by a beautiful miniature botanical garden *(see p59)*.

⑩ Parque El Capricho
Paseo de la Alameda de Osuna 25 ▪ **Metro El Capricho** ▪ **Open 9am–6:30pm Sat, Sun & public hols (Apr–Sep: to 9pm)** ▪ **Closed 1 Jan, 25 Dec** ▪ **www.reservaspatrimonio.es**

These 18th-century gardens belonged to the palace of the Duke and Duchess of Osuna and were landscaped by Jean-Baptiste Mulot, the gardener at the palace of Versailles, outside Paris. They have been restored to their former glory with tree-lined paths, fountains, a lake and follies. Housed in the park is the Civil War Bunker, that can be visited by reservation.

Temple of Bacchus, Parque El Capricho

Following pages Tropical garden in the 19th-century Invernadero de Atocha

🔟 Sporting Venues

The impressive exterior of the Estadio Santiago Bernabéu

1 Estadio Santiago Bernabéu

Avenida de Concha Espina 1 ■ **Metro Santiago Bernabéu** ■ **Stadium Tour: daily except 1 Jan & 25 Dec** ■ **Adm (under 4s free)** ■ **www.realmadrid. com/estadio-santiago-bernabeu**

This stadium was named after the president and former player, Santiago Bernabéu, who oversaw its construction. Real Madrid, recognised by FIFA as the 'Best Club of the 20th Century', has won more than 90 trophies in both domestic and international competitions since its formation in 1902. A stadium tour allows visitors to view these trophies up close and also includes a panoramic view of the

81,044-seater stadium, a tour of the team changing rooms and grounds, as well as an audiovisual and interactive display about the club.

2 Wanda Metropolitano

Avenida de Luis Aragones, 4 ■ **Metro Estadio Metropolitano** ■ **Guided tours: check website** ■ **Adm** ■ **www.atleticodemadrid.com/ wandametropolitano**

Real Madrid's arch-rivals, Atlético de Madrid, play in this 68,000 seat stadium, in San Blas. For most of its history, the club has lived in the shadow of Real Madrid, but all is forgotten when the two clash in annual matches, billed as the "duel of the gods". The club's best season was in 1996 when it won a league and cup, but four years later the club suffered the humiliation of being relegated to the second division. King Felipe VI has been the Honorary President since 2003. In 2017, the club moved here from its previous stadium, The Estadio Vicente Calderon.

3 WiZink Center

Avenida Felipe II ■ **Metro Goya, O'Donnell or Príncipe de Vergara** ■ **www.wizinkcenter.es**

Inaugurated in February 2005, the WiZink Center (previously known as the Palacio de los Deportes, or Sports Palace) occupies the site

of a former sports centre that was destroyed by fire in 2001. The building seats 18,000 spectators and was designed to accommodate several sports including athletics, basketball, handball, tennis and boxing. As well as improving both safety and security measures, the centre's acoustics were enhanced in order to make it suitable for pop and rock concerts.

4 Las Ventas
Calle de Alcalá 237 ■ Metro Ventas ■ www.las-ventas.com
Although controversial, bullfighting has been an integral part of Spanish tradition for centuries. *Corridas* (fights) in Madrid take place annually from March to December in the Las Ventas stadium, one of the largest bullrings in the world. It houses a museum which portrays the historic and cultural significance of bullfighting. Tours of the arena and museum are available all year round.

5 Jogging Spots
Most *Madrileños* head for the Retiro, Jardines Sabatini, Casa de Campo or Madrid Río Park and Paseo Pintor Rosales with views of the Parque del Oeste *(see p52)*.

6 Outdoor Swimming Pools
www.esmadrid.com/en/summer-pools
Madrid's outdoor swimming pools are open from June to mid-September. The Casa de Campo *(see p53)*, which has three pools – children's, intermediate and Olympic-sized – where visitors can unwind. Children and adults can also cool off at Urban Beach in Madrid Rio.

7 Hipódromo de la Zarzuela
Avenida Padre Huidobro, Road A-6, 8km ■ 917 40 05 40 ■ Opening times vary ■ Closed Jan & Feb ■ Adm (spring & fall: under 18s free; summer: under 14s free) ■ www.hipodromo delazarzuela.es
Tickets for horse racing can be booked in advance online, by phone or in person at the racetrack on Sundays, 11:30am–3pm. Visit the stables before racing begins to pick the favourite, and enjoy live music after the winner is announced.

8 Madrid Caja Mágica
Parque Lineal del Manzanares, Camino de Perales 23 ■ Metro San Fermín-Orcasur ■ Opening times vary according to events being held there
This hi-tech sports complex, designed by architect Dominique Perrault, is dedicated to tennis. It includes 11 indoor and 16 outdoor tennis courts.

9 Circuito del Jarama
Circuito del Jarama, Road A-1, 28km ■ Bus No. 166 from Plaza Castilla ■ www.jarama.org
Fans of *automovilísmo* (motor racing) or *motociclísmo* (motorcycle racing) should head to this track, close to San Sebastián de los Reyes, 28 km (17 miles) northeast of Madrid. Race meetings are held here throughout the summer, with a range of activities available, including karting and driving courses. Booking is essential.

Club de Campo Villa de Madrid

10 Club de Campo Villa de Madrid
Carretera de Castilla 2km ■ Bus Nos. 160, 161 and A from Moncloa ■ www.ccvm.es
Golf is big business in Spain, due to the interest generated by the likes of champions José María Olazábal and the late Severiano Ballesteros. Even though it is a barren terrain, several 18-hole courses are in the Greater Madrid area. The Club de Campo was designed by Javier Arana in 1957 and is one of the best in Europe.

🔟 Off the Beaten Track

Parque Quinta de los Molinos

1 Parque Quinta de los Molinos

MAP B1 ▪ Calle Alcalá 527 ▪ Open 6:30am–10pm daily ▪ Metro Suanzes

Every spring, almond trees blossom in clouds of pink and white in this pretty park, which dates from 1920.

2 Hammam Al Ándalus

MAP N5 ▪ Calle Atocha, 14 ▪ 914 29 90 20 ▪ Open 10am–10pm daily; closed 25 Dec ▪ Adm ▪ www. madrid.hammamalandalus.com

Recover from museum-fever and tramping the Madrid pavements in this hammam, which has soothing Andalus-style decor, warm baths and a massage service.

3 Museo del Aire (Museo de Aeronáutica y Astronáutica de España)

MAP A2 ▪ Aeródromo de Cuatro Vientos, Autovia A5, km 10, 700 ▪ All buses on the Madrid-Alcorcón-Móstoles route from Príncipe Pío station; Metro Cuatro Vientos, then walk 1 km or take a bus ▪ 915 09 16 90 ▪ Open 10am–2pm Tue–Sun ▪ www.ejercitodelaire.mde.es

The Spanish Air Force's museum contains one of the largest collections of vintage aircraft in Europe. There are helicopters, jet fighters and more, including a Breguet 19 that crossed the Southern Atlantic Ocean in 1929.

4 CentroCentro

MAP F4 ▪ Plaza Cibeles 1 ▪ 914 80 00 08 ▪ www.centrocentro.org

The chill-out lounge in CentroCentro (see p82) is set in what was once the main hall of Madrid's opulent former post office (and now city hall). With a wide selection of newspapers and magazines, it's the ideal spot to relax before hitting the nearby Museo Nacional del Prado (see pp16–21). Book ahead for guided tours of the original early 20th-century palace.

5 Matadero Madrid – Centro de Creación Contemporánea

MAP B2 ▪ Plaza de Legazpi 8 ▪ Metro Legazpi; bus 6, 8, 18, 19, 45, 78 & 148 ▪ 915 17 73 09 ▪ Opening times vary, check website ▪ Adm for films and some activities ▪ www. mataderomadrid.org

Located in a beautifully converted former slaughterhouse, this cultural centre is dedicated to the creative output of contemporary artists, and features cutting-edge exhibitions, film screenings at the Cineteca and more. It also has a fantastic café, bar, restaurant and a bicycle hire service.

Real Fábrica de Tapices of Madrid

6 Real Fábrica de Tapices

Housed in an elegant Neomudéjar-style building, the fascinating Royal Tapestry Factory *(see p82)* is located in the Paseo del Prado area. Watch exquisite wall-hangings and carpets being made using traditional methods and admire antique looms at this factory, which was founded in 1721 by Felipe V. It also contains a superb collection of historic textiles created for Spanish monarchs over the centuries.

7 Museo La Neomudéjar

MAP H6 ▪ Calle Antonio Nebrija ▪ Open 11am–3pm & 5–9pm Wed–Sun ▪ www.laneomudejar.com

Located next to Atocha train station in the former offices of the state railway company, this trendy avant-garde arts centre hosts changing exhibitions of paintings, murals, installation art, video art and sculptures by young artists. It also has a year-round roster of workshops, talks and art festivals.

8 Museo del Ferrocarril

Set in the 19th-century Delicias train station, this museum *(see p82)* is packed with steam engines, period carriages, model trains and lots more to amuse all ages. Even the café is set in a delightful carriage from the 1920s. On second weekends, it hosts Mercado de Motores, a flea market featuring more than 200 designers, artisans, artists and musicians. The museum is also the starting point for the Tren de la Fresa *(see p61)*.

9 Andén 0

MAP E1 ▪ Plaza de Chamberí s/n ▪ 913 92 06 93 ▪ Closed until further notice due to COVID-19

Madrid has its very own underground "ghost station"– the Chamberí metro stop (its new name means "Platform Zero") – which was closed in 1966 and hasn't changed since, except to fall into disrepair. Now lovingly restored to its former glory, it is a small and interesting museum, with exhibits that recall its history and use as a bomb shelter during the Civil War.

10 Roof terrace at the Círculo de Bellas Artes

A sumptuous 1920s art club and cultural centre, the Círculo de Bellas Artes *(see p94)* has a hidden gem – its wonderful roof terrace, which can be accessed by a glass lift. Once up on the roof, you can enjoy fabulous city-wide views. It is the perfect spot for late-evening cocktails, and occasional live music as well. Note that the roof terrace is sometimes closed for private events, so check in advance. Entry also includes admission to the beautiful café, La Pecera *(see p99)*.

Círculo de Bellas Artes roof terrace

TOP 10 Children's Attractions

Exhibits at Museo Natural de Ciencias

1 Museo Natural de Ciencias

Calle de José Gutiérrez Abascal 2 ■ Open 10am–5pm Tue–Fri (Aug: to 3pm), 10am–8pm Sat, Sun & public hols ■ Closed 1 & 6 Jan, 1 May & 25 Dec ■ Adm ■ www.mncn.csic.es

Opened in 1771, this museum houses one of Europe's oldest natural history collections, with specimens including fossils, dinosaurs, sharks and birds. Children's workshops are held at the museum throughout the year.

2 Parque de Atracciones

Casa de Campo ■ Parque de Atracciones ■ Metro Batán ■ Open times vary, check website ■ Adm (free for children under 100 cm/ 39 inches in height) ■ www.parque deatracciones.es/horarios

This amusement park features stomach-churning rides, fun-filled diversions such as puppet and magic shows, and a virtual reality zone. The rides include Los Rápidos (a chance to try white-water rafting) and Top Spin. For the very young, and the more faint-hearted, there are merry-go-rounds and train and boat rides.

3 Faunia

Avenida de las Comunidades 28 ■ Valdebernardo ■ Metro Valdebernardo ■ Opening times vary, check website ■ Adm (under 3s free) ■ www.faunia.es/horarios

All areas of this botanical garden and zoological park have been designed to recreate a different ecosystem with captivating sights, sounds and smells. Visitors can "experience" a tropical storm, journey to the polar regions and observe nocturnal creatures in their natural habitat.

4 Parque Warner

Camino de la Warner, San Martin de la Vega ■ Road A-4, exit (salida) 22 ■ Train C-3A from Estación del Arte ■ Opening times vary, check website ■ Adm (free for children under 100 cm/ 39 inches in height) ■ www.parquewarner.com

This amusement park is divided into multiple themed areas: Superheroes is devoted to the fantasy worlds of Gotham City and Metrópolis, and The Wild West recalls Hollywood Westerns of the John Wayne era. You can also tour the replicated film sets of the Warner Brothers Studio.

5 Palacio de Hielo

Calle Silvano 77 ■ Metro Canillas ■ 91 716 0400 ■ Opening times vary, check website ■ Shops: open 10am–10pm Mon–Sat, noon–8pm Sun & public hols; closed 1 & 6 Jan, 1 May, 25 Dec ■ Adm ■ www.palaciodehielo.com

Located in the heart of Madrid, Palacio de Hielo is a retail, leisure and entertainment complex with

an Olympic-sized (1,800-sq m/ 2,150-sq yd) ice rink. Skates can be available for hire and classes can be taken. It has various other amenities, including 12 restaurants and cafés, a children's playground, a bowling alley, a 15-screen cinema and a gym.

Food court, Centro Comercial Xanadú

⑥ Centro Comercial Xanadú

Road A-5, exit (salida) 22 ▪ Bus 528, 534, 539, 541, 545, 546, 547 & 548 from Príncipe Pío ▪ Shops: open 10am–10pm daily; closed 1 & 6 Jan, 25 Dec; Cinema and Snow Park: open 9–1am daily (to 2am Fri & Sat) ▪ www.intuxanadu.com

A shopping mall and entertainment centre that houses the Madrid Snow Zone, this place also features an indoor ski slope and ski school, cinemas, restaurants, bowling and go-karting. It is also home to the Atlantis Aquarium and Nickelodeon Adventure theme park.

⑦ Aquópolis

Avenida de la Dehesa s/n Villanueva de la Cañada ▪ Opening times vary, check website ▪ Adm ▪ www.villanueva.aquopolis.es

A range of giant water slides, toboggans, cascades and spirals is on offer at Madrid's vast water park. There's also a lake, wave pool and toddlers' paddling pool, as well as cafés and restaurants.

⑧ Tren de la Fresa

MAP A3 ▪ Train from Museo del Ferrocarril ▪ 912 32 03 20 ▪ Opening times vary, call ahead ▪ Adm (free for children under 100 cm/ 39 inches in height)

Great fun for the kids and a nostalgic journey into the past for the grown-ups, the "Strawberry Train" is pulled by an old steam locomotive. It follows the original route from Madrid to Aranjuez, which first opened in 1850. Hostesses in period costume serve Aranjuez's famous strawberries. There are various ticket options, ranging from a round trip ticket to a complete tour ticket, which includes entry to the palace.

⑨ Teleférico

MAP A2 ▪ Paseo del Pintor Rosales ▪ Open from noon, closing times vary, check website ▪ Adm (under 4s free) ▪ www.teleferico madrid.es

The cable car ride between Parque del Oeste and Casa de Campo is enjoyable for both kids and parents. There are fabulous views of the city skyline – the leaflet inside the cable car will help you locate major landmarks such as the Palacio Real.

The Teleférico across Casa de Campo

⑩ Parque del Retiro

The Retiro's *(see pp36–7)* central location makes it an ideal place to visit if the children are in the mood to run wild. On weekends (times vary), take them to the puppet show in the open-air theatre near the lake. They won't need to know any Spanish as the fun is infectious.

Entertainment Venues

1 Centro Cultural Conde Duque

MAP C2 ■ Calle del Conde Duque 11 ■ www.condeduquemadrid.es

For most of the year this cultural centre (see p72) hosts temporary art exhibitions. During the annual Summer Arts Festival (see p74), opera, plays and concerts are on the programme, with many events staged outdoors.

2 Cine Doré

MAP E5 ■ Calle de Santa Isabel 3 ■ www.culturaydeporte.gob.es

This beautiful 1920s cinema is now the headquarters of the Spanish National Film Institute. There are two screens showing an excellent selection of classic and contemporary films in the original version, and at very reasonable prices. During the summer, films are also shown on an outdoor screen on the terrace (book ahead). The café in the foyer is a good place to meet up with friends.

3 Teatro Real

Since its renovation in the 1990s, Madrid's splendid opera house (see p102) now seats up to 1,750 spectators. It has earned its international acclaim as one of the most iconic cultural venues for classical operas, performed by international and Spanish companies. The season runs from September to July and audio guide tours are available in multiple languages, if you want to look around this spectacular building.

4 Teatro de la Zarzuela

MAP E4 ■ Calle de Jovellanos 4 ■ www.teatrodelazarzuela.mcu.es

The beautiful Teatro de la Zarzuela dates from 1856 and was built especially to stage zarzuela, a form of light opera unique to Spain. After decades of neglect, zarzuela is seeing a revival and the theatre commissions new works from time to time, as well as performing classics such as The Barber of Lavapiés and The Pharaoh's Court. The season runs from September to June. During the summer, the theatre is used for flamenco and ballet performances.

5 Teatro Fernán Gómez

MAP G2 ■ Plaza de Colón 4 ■ www.teatrofernangomez.es

Events at this important arts centre range from temporary art exhibitions to ballet, jazz, dramatic plays, zarzuela and experimental theatre.

Elegant façade of the Teatro Real

Casa de América

6 Casa de América
MAP F3 ■ Plaza de Cibeles s/n
■ www.casamerica.es

The Neo-Baroque Palacio de Linares, a marvellous architectural monument in its own right, dominating the southern end of the Paseo de Recoletos, is now a major cultural centre showcasing Latin American arts. It offers a regular programme of films, exhibitions and concerts, plus a good bookshop, café and the Cien Llaves restaurant.

7 Fundación Juan March
Fans of modern art will enjoy the world-class temporary exhibitions held here *(see p86)*. The cultural and scientific foundation also sponsors lunchtime chamber concerts on weekdays, usually starting around noon (the monthly programme is available from the centre). While here, take a look at some of the modern sculptures in the forecourt such as *Meeting Place* (1975) by Eduardo Chillida.

8 Sala Riviera
MAP A4 ■ Paseo Bajo de la Virgen del Puerto ■ www.salariviera.com

If you're interested in hearing pop and rock acts such as Metronomy, Noel Gallagher or Fontaines D.C, this is where they're most likely to perform while in Madrid. Acoustics and visibility are both good (better than many venues) and fans can cool off in the summer when the roof is drawn back. It is also a popular club, featuring local and international DJs.

9 Teatro Monumental
MAP E5 ■ Calle de Atocha 65
■ www.rtve.es

Designed by Teodoro Anasagasti in 1922, and remodelled in 2018, this theatre, known for its acoustics, is the home of both the RTVE orchestra and choir (Spain's state radio and television company), as well as the acclaimed Madrid Symphony Orchestra.

10 Auditorio Nacional de Música
Calle del Príncipe de Vergara 146
■ Metro Prosperidad, Cruz del Rayo
■ www.auditorionacional.mcu.es

This modern concert hall, in a residential district north of the centre, is home to the National Orchestra of Spain, and the major venue for symphony concerts from October to June. The Orchestra of the Comunidad de Madrid also performs here, as do a number of international ensembles.

🔟 Bars

Photographs of celebrity customers on the wall at Museo Chicote

❶ Museo Chicote

In the 1930s, "the best bar in Spain" was Ernest Hemingway's verdict on this cocktail bar *(see p98)*. It was in the 1950s and 1960s, however, that Chicote became really famous, thanks to visiting celebrities such as Frank Sinatra. The bar is at its best in the late evening.

❷ Bodega de la Ardosa

This popular watering hole *(see p125)* has a pedigree going back more than 100 years. Welcoming guests since 1892, the pub was given a makeover in the 1980s and the owner claims it was the first bar in Madrid to celebrate St Patrick's night. That was when they started serving Guinness and home-made *tortilla*, one of the mainstays of an enticing tapas menu. Today, La Ardosa is a popular place to enjoy a vermouth alongside an amiable clientele.

❸ Café Manuela

"Manuela" refers to Manuela Malasaña *(see p120)*. The statue of the local heroine is a feature of the lovely late 19th-century decor, which includes mirrors, fluted columns and stucco flourishes. The entertainment here *(see p124)* ranges from concerts and poetry readings (sometimes bilingual) to discussions and exhibitions by local artists. The friendly staff serves coffee, beer, cocktails and tapas depending on the time of day.

❹ Radio Rooftop

With stylish sofas and custom-designed hanging lights, this rooftop terrace and bar *(see p116)* has some of the most outstanding views of the city, plus great cocktails and a

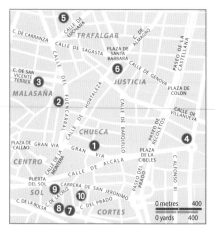

good selection of music. A quieter lounge can be found inside, along with a VIP bar that is frequented by glamorous celebrities.

Sala Clamores

Once a classic jazz café, this bar *(see p124)* is now one of the best-known places in Madrid to enjoy live music. Listen to jazz, blues, funk, or tango performances by renowned artists while sipping cocktails at this large, yet intimate club.

6 Cervecería Santa Bárbara

A Madrid institution, this large beer hall *(see p125)* is the perfect place to unwind after a day's sightseeing, or to begin a night on the town. Both dark beer and lager are available on draught – some *Madrileños* like to mix the two.

7 Cervecería Alemana

This beer and tapas bar *(see p117)* owes a good deal of its popularity to its terrace on Plaza Santa Ana. Like Museo Chicote, the Alemana was a favourite of Ernest Hemingway and other famous expats. It serves both Spanish and imported beers.

8 Restaurante Ramses.Life

Swing by at 1am and spot Ferraris parked outside this Philippe Starck-designed complex. Popular with Madrid's fashionistas, this large cocktail bar *(see p91)* is perfect for people-watching, not forgetting

the extensive drinks menu. There are also two restaurants and a base-ment club. The weekend brunch is a good hangover cure; choose a table with a plaza view.

Guests sitting at the bar at Alhambra

9 Alhambra

Designed to look like a bar from the early 1900s with lovely Moorish touches, Alhambra *(see p116)* is one of the best places to start the evening if you're about to embark on a tour of the night spots of Sol and Santa Ana. Check out the Andalucían tapas, especially the cured meats and spicy sausage. As well as beer and sangria, there's also a good selection of Spanish wine available.

10 La Venencia

A bar for sherry drinkers who know their fino from their manzanilla, La Venencia *(see p116)* opened its doors in 1929 and still does a roaring trade, especially in the evenings when tourists mingle with a loyal local following. The decor is ageing as gra-ciously as the sherries behind the counter, and there is a good selection of canapés and tapas such as *mojama* (sliced, salt-cured tuna). It is as forbidden to tip, as it is to spit on the floor. Note that the bar serves sherry only.

Restaurante Ramses.Life

🔟 Tapas Bars

① Tasca La Farmacia
Like all genuine Madrid *tascas*, this pub *(see p90)* on the edge of Salamanca serves its customers a tasty appetizer with each drink, to give them an idea of what's on offer. *Croquetas de Bacalao* – béchamel paste deep-fried with nuggets of cod – are the house speciality.

Interiors of Taberna del Alabardero

② Taberna del Alabardero
Located in the vicinity of Teatro Real, this little *taberna (see p105)* opened its doors in 1974 and has been delighting its clientele ever since. Try the Basque cuisine that the chefs make with fresh vegetables straight from the garden.

③ Venta El Buscón

A traditional tapas bar *(see p116)*, Venta El Buscón is decorated with artisan tiles and paintings of the Spanish poet Quevedo. It serves typical tapas *Madrileñas* at excellent prices, with a variety of fish and meat dishes. Don't miss the Spanish omelette or the fried squid.

④ Los Gatos
Bring your camera when you visit this wonderfully over-the-top bar *(see p83)*, often overlooked by tourists. Every inch of space is crammed with bric-a-brac – signed basketball shirts, old telephones, beer barrels, bulls' heads and countless other curiosities. Steer your way to the bar for a glass of beer and a plate of shrimps. While you are there, take a look at the tempting array of canapés, filled rolls and delicious tapas.

⑤ Taberna Antonio Sánchez
This Lavapiés hostelry *(see p117)* dates from 1786. The wooden furniture and bullfighting memorabilia are as traditional as the menu of tortilla and stews.

The bar at Taberna Antonio Sánchez

La Casa del Abuelo

Near Plaza Santa Ana, "Grandad's Place" is an atmospheric spit-and-sawdust bar *(see p117)*. It's customary to order the house wine with the tapas – variations around the humble shrimp. Try them grilled in their shells *(a la plancha)* or peeled and sautéed in oil and garlic *(al ajillo)*. Standing room only.

La Perejila

A local favourite, this cosy bar *(see p116)* features Andalucian decor.

Classic tapas dishes prepared with an innovative twist and an excellent range of wines are available here. Popular dishes include veal meatballs; smoked cod; tomato purée with bread, olive oil, vinegar and garlic, and warm toast with grapes and almonds.

Traditional shrimp tapas

Bodegas Rosell

Embellished with colourful *Madrileño*-style tiles, this early 20th-century tavern *(see p83)* is owned by the award-winning sommelier Manolo Rosell. The menu features tasty traditional tapas that can be paired with a choice of wine from the extensive wine list.

Casa Gonzalez

Founded in 1931, this hybrid gourmet cheese shop and tapas joint *(see p116)* is known for its choice of dishes and wines. The menu here features superb charcuterie, canned fish and seafood, among other delicacies. Get a few tapas with a bottle of wine and sit at a marble table by the window to savour them.

Casa Labra

Do not miss out on the cod and cod croquettes here *(see p98)*. If you don't fancy standing at the bar, classic Madrid dishes are served in the gorgeous 19th-century, wood-panelled room at the back.

TOP 10 SPANISH TAPAS DISHES

Deep-fried croquetas

1 Croquetas
Spanish croquettes are made with a thick béchamel sauce and chopped ham, cod or spinach, then deep-fried.

2 Canapés
The toppings for canapés range from anchovies and egg slices to *morcilla* (black pudding) and smoked salmon.

3 Tortilla
The famous Spanish omelette is far thicker than those of other cuisines and is made with sliced potatoes and onions.

4 Pimientos
Peppers are usually served *rellenos* (stuffed with meat, cod or tuna) or *pimientos de padrón* – grilled and salted.

5 Empanadillas
These are small pastries usually with tuna and tomato or meat fillings.

6 Potato dishes
These include *patatas bravas* (fried, with a spicy tomato sauce) or *patatas alioli* (boiled, with a mayonnaise and garlic dressing).

7 Raciones
Larger dishes to share, including hot stews, *jamón serrano* (cured ham), *chorizo* (spicy sausage) and *queso manchego* (sheep's milk cheese).

8 Conservas
Canned fish, including *boquerones* (anchovies), *mejillones* (mussels) and *berberechos* (cockles).

9 Soldaditos de Pavía
These are cod sticks fried in batter.

10 Gambas
Shrimps are grilled in their shells *(a la plancha)* or peeled and then sautéed in olive oil and garlic *(al ajillo)*.

🔟 Restaurants

Historic interior of Sobrino de Botín

① Sobrino de Botín

According to the *Guinness World Records*, Botín *(see p117)* is the world's oldest restaurant, having opened its doors in 1725. The dining rooms retain much of their original decor including *azulejos* (tiles) and oak beams, and the atmosphere is convivial. Botín is famous for Castilian fare and the house speciality, roast suckling pig.

② DiverXO

Chef David Muñoz, who trained at London's Hakkasan and Nobu, was awarded a third Michelin star in 2013 for his exceptional Spanish–Asian fusion cuisine at DiverXO *(see p91)*. Try the 12 course-tasting menu which presents mind-bending experimental dishes made with the best of local ingredients. The restaurant seats only 32 people so booking is essential.

③ Santceloni

This sleek former outpost of the late Catalan chef Santi Santamaria is one of the city's finest restaurants *(see p91)*, with two Michelin stars. The menu features superbly prepared, dishes, such as kid with roasted pumpkin, black garlic and hazelnuts. Booking is essential.

④ Lhardy

A Madrid institution, founded in 1839, Lhardy's *(see p99)* upstairs dining rooms are wonderfully intimate and more than an elegant touch with *belle époque* gilded mirrors, wainscoting, Limoges china and Bohemian crystal. The cooking is *Madrileño* rather than French and the house speciality is *cocido* (chickpea stew).

⑤ Casa Lucio

A family restaurant *(see p116)* and a meeting point for locals with more than 40 years of history, Casa Lucio is located in the premises of Mesón El Segoviano, where chef Lucio Blázquez began work at the age of 12. Enjoy traditional Spanish dishes made with the best local ingredients – try the delicious egg dish and stews.

⑥ Viridiana

Named after the Buñuel film, this cosy modern *locale (see p83)* is located between Paseo del Prado and Retiro Park, and is the life's work of its inspired and inspiring chef, Abraham García. This is the perfect restaurant for a special occasion: the menu is imaginative, the dishes are exquisitely presented and the wine list is superb.

7 Restaurante La Trainera

Named after the long row boats in the Bay of Biscay, where the restaurant has a fishing vessel, Restaurante La Trainera *(see p91)* has expanded into a labyrinth of rooms with pine tables and chairs. The menu uses a variety of seafood, not only from the Bay of Biscay, but from Cádiz and the Mediterranean as well. Try the shellfish salad.

8 Estado Puro

Savour award-winning gastronomic tapas at this funky, informal establishment *(see p83)* run by famed Spanish chef, Paco Roncero. The menu incorporates molecular gastronomy and fusion cuisine to create a medley of sub-lime flavours and an array of small dishes to mix and match. Try the delicious asparagus tempura.

Well-lit interiors of Estado Puro

9 Ramón Freixa Madrid

Imaginative chef Ramón Freixa blends tradition with innovation in his two-star Michelin restaurant *(see p91)*. Choose one of the three tasting menus or from the à la carte selection.

10 BiBo Andalusian Brasserie & Tapas

With three Michelin stars to his name, Dani García's tapas bar *(see p91)* won't disappoint. Take a culinary trip around the world with some 80 international dishes and an impressive cellar.

TOP 10 SPANISH DISHES

1 Cocido Madrileño
This classic Madrid stew might include pigs' trotters, beef shank, chicken, sausage, chickpeas and vegetables.

2 Cochinillo Asado
The Castilian countryside is famous for its suckling pig, slow-roasted in a wood-fired oven until the meat is tender and the skin is crispy.

3 Callos a la Madrileña
Tripe may not be to everyone's taste, but try it "Madrid-style", with *chorizo*, tomatoes, onions and paprika.

4 Bacalao
There are many ways of cooking salted cod. Ernest Hemingway relished *bacalao al ajoarriero*, a cod stew made with tomatoes, peppers and garlic.

5 Gazpacho
Hailing from Andalucía, this famous cold soup's main ingredients are tomatoes, garlic, cucumber, olive oil, green peppers and vinegar.

6 Pulpo a la Gallega
Octopus "Galician style" comes in slices on a layer of potato, with a large dose of olive oil and a sprinkling of paprika.

7 Fabada Asturiana
This white bean stew is served piping hot with *morcilla* (black pudding).

8 Txangurro
Spider crab is a Basque delicacy served mixed with other seafood in its shell.

9 Merluza Rebozada
Another north country favourite is hake fried in breadcrumbs.

10 Paella
The most famous Spanish rice dish is traditionally cooked with rabbit and chicken, but today it is more common to find seafood variations.

Seafood Paella

🔟 Classic Spanish Shops

1 Patrimonio Comunal Olivarero

Spain is the largest producer of olive oil in the world and this representative *(see p123)* of a grower's cooperative knows his business. As with wines, it is possible to distinguish different varieties of oils by colour, flavour and smell, and tastings here are part of the fun.

2 Capas Seseña

This family-run firm *(see p113)* near Sol has been making traditional full-length Spanish *capas* (capes) since 1901, hand-tailored from the finest wool. Famous clients over the years have included Rudolph Valentino, Hillary Clinton and Bruce Springsteen, alongside Spanish royalty. Needless to say, a made-to-measure cape of this quality does not come cheap.

Exterior of Capas Seseña

3 El Ángel

Religion still plays an important role in Spanish life, and Madrid is famous for its characterful shops specializing in devotional objects. Founded in 1867, family-run El Ángel *(see p113)* furnishes churches and monasteries across the country. The shop is a veritable museum, with over 1000 sq m (3281 sq ft) of articles, including rosaries, statues, paintings, icons and communion cups.

Manuel González Contreras guitar

4 Guitarras Manuel Contreras

One of Spain's most respected guitar workshops *(see p104)* was founded in 1962. Clients have ranged from the classical virtuoso Andrés Segovia to pop guitarist Mark Knopfler. There's a small museum of instruments dating back to the 19th century, and it's fascinating to see the craftsmen at work.

5 Flamencoexport

If you've been won over by flamenco during your stay, now is your chance to look the part. This specialist store *(see p104)* has everything – colourful costumes and accessories such as fans, flowers and ornamental combs, as well as guitars, books, sheet music, videos, records and CDs.

6 Antigua Casa Talavera

Dating back to the early 20th century, Antigua Casa Talavera *(see p104)* sells ceramics that are handmade by Spanish potters. Regional styles are represented from all the major centres of ceramics production in Spain, including the famous blue

A painted tile

and yellow designs from Talavera de Reina. Items include decorative tiles, plates, vases, sangria pitchers and reproductions of museum pieces.

7 Franjul

Designing and crafting handbags and shoes since 1947, Franjul *(see p113)* embodies Spanish style with its bespoke accessories. Here, you can choose from a wide selection of styles and materials to create your own one-of-a-kind handbag or a pair of shoes.

8 Casa Mira

This old-fashioned shop *(see p113)* has been producing its famous nougat *(turrón)* for more than 150 years. Made without artificial colourings or preservatives, it's the genuine article.

Liquor at Bodegas Mariano Madrueño

9 Bodegas Mariano Madrueño

This centenarian liquor shop *(see p114)* offers an extensive selection of wines, vermouths and brandies. Sometimes, they host wine tasting sessions, and have live music.

10 Taller Puntera
MAP C4 ▪ Plaza del Conde de Barajas 4 ▪ 913 642 926 ▪ www. puntera.com/gb

Located between Plaza Mayor and Plaza de la Villa, this workshop and store sells unique handcrafted leather objects. Visitors can also attend workshops introducing them to the basics of leather work; slots can be booked online.

TOP 10 SPANISH MARKETS

Mercado de la Cebada

1 Mercado de la Cebada
MAP C5 ▪ Plaza de la Cebada s/n ▪ Open 9am–6pm Sat, 11am–5pm 1st Sun of the month
This food market's origins date back to 1875 when it was opened by King Alfonso XII *(see p114)*.

2 Ferias de Artesanía
Craft fairs are put up between 1–30 December. Try Plaza Mayor *(see pp22–3)*.

3 Mercado de Vallehermoso
MAP C1 ▪ Calle de Vallehermoso 36 ▪ Open 9am–11pm Mon–Thu (to midnight Fri & Sat, 12:30pm–5pm Sun
Housed in a 1930s building, this food market is full of local produce.

4 El Rastro
This famous flea market takes place every Sunday morning *(see pp26–7)*.

5 Mercado de Maravillas
Calle Bravo Murillo 122 ▪ Metro Alvarado ▪ Open Mon–Fri & Sat am
Fresh fruit and vegetables, bread, cured ham and cheese.

6 Mercado de Chamartín
Calle Bolivia 9 ▪ Metro Colombia ▪ Open Mon–Fri (closed at midday) & Sat am
Fish and gourmet products.

7 Mercado de San Miguel
Delicatessen stalls selling food and drink to enjoy on site *(see p105)*.

8 Mercado de la Paz
The main attraction of this small market *(see p88)* is the cheese stalls.

9 Mercado de San Antón
MAP R1 ▪ Calle Augusto Figueroa 24 ▪ Open Mon–Sat
Flowers, food and wine *(see p121)*.

10 Librerías de la Cuesta de Moyano
MAP F6 ▪ Calle de Claudio Moyano ▪ Open late May–mid-Jun: Mon–Sun (closed at midday)
Old, new and second-hand books.

⭐10 Madrid for Free

Madrid Río waterside park on the banks of the Manzanares River

1 Madrid Río
■ Metro Príncipe Pío & Puerta del Ángel ■ www.esmadrid.com/en/tourist-information/madrid-rio/

This contemporary park near the Puente de Segovia follows the banks of the Manzanares River, and offers gardens, children's play areas, bicycle and jogging paths, plus viewing points, fountains and bridges. There's also a skate park, a climbing wall and facilities for playing basketball, pétanque and paddle tennis. In summer it even has its own beach, which attracts *Madrileños* in droves.

Entrance to Centro Cultural Conde Duque

2 Paseo del Arte Museums
Madrid's world-class museums all offer free entry at specific times. The Prado (see pp16–21) is free Mondays to Saturdays from 6–8pm and on Sundays from 5–7pm. The Museo Nacional Thyssen-Bornemisza (see pp28–31) is free on Mondays from noon to 4pm, and the Museo Nacional Centro de Arte Reina Sofía (see pp32–5) is free Mondays and Wednesdays to Saturdays from 7–9pm and on Sundays from 1:30–7pm.

3 Local Festivals
The biggest festival in Madrid is held in honour of the city's patron saint, San Isidro (see p74), and takes place for a week around 15 May. Locals, dressed in traditional costume, head to the Parque de San Isidro for outdoor concerts, picnics and food and drink stalls that line the streets. There are plenty of traditional festivals throughout the year, including the Fiestas del Dos de Mayo, held for a week around 2 May in Malasaña, and the Verbena la Paloma which takes place in La Latina in August.

4 Centro Cultural Conde Duque
This city-run cultural centre (see p62) is home to Madrid's Contemporary Art Museum, and also features an auditorium, a library and several exhibition spaces. All exhibitions, including those in the Contemporary Art Museum, are free. A regular programme of talks, workshops and kid-friendly activities is on offer.

5 La Casa Encendida
MAP E6 ■ Ronda de Valencia 2 ■ 915 06 21 80 ■ Open 10am–10pm Tue–Sun ■ www.lacasaencendida.es

This fantastic cultural centre, run by a private foundation, offers a wide range of free exhibitions, workshops, courses and family-friendly activities, and has a charming rooftop garden with fabulous views over the city.

⑥ Gran Vía
MAP D3

Enjoy the fascinating part of the city centre by indulging in Spanish gastronomy and exploring splendid buildings, such as Edificio Metropolis.

⑦ Palacio de Cristal
MAP G4 ■ Puerta de Alcalá ■ **Open Apr–Sep: 10am–10pm daily; 24 & 31 Dec: 10am–5pm** ■ Closed 1 & 6 Jan, 1 May, 25 Dec

The glass palace in Parque del Retiro (see pp36–7) has been converted into one of Madrid's most beautiful galleries. It hosts temporary exhibitions run by the Museo Nacional Centro de Arte Reina Sofía (see pp32–5). Due to the palace's unusual construction, there are no visits on rainy days.

⑧ Parque Juan Carlos I
Madrileños come here (see p53) to stroll, cycle (free bicycles are available by the hour) and picnic. There are playgrounds, a little train and free activities on weekends.

The verdant Parque Juan Carlos I

⑨ Planetario de Madrid
Parque Tierno Galván, Av del Planetario 16 ■ Metro Mendez Alvaro ■ **914 67 34 61** ■ **Opening times vary, check website** ■ www.planetmad.es

While the planetarium's projection shows charge admission, you can visit the exhibition galleries, which have fascinating interactive and audio-visual exhibits, for free.

⑩ Municipal Museums
Many offer free admission, such as the Museo de Arte Público, Museo de los Orígenes (see p107) and Museo de Historia de Madrid (see p119).

TOP 10 BUDGET TIPS

Madrid Metro sign

1 The Bono Metrobus pass allows you to make 10 metro or bus journeys for €12.20.

2 Fill up with a *menú del día* (set-price lunch) or *plato combinado* (dish of the day) on weekday lunchtimes for around €14.

3 An Abono Turístico travel pass is ideal if you are using public transport extensively: valid for 1–7 days, it costs from €8.40.

4 If you won't be leaving central Madrid, consider getting around on foot, which is a healthier option to using public transport and a good way of saving money.

5 Buy your picnic supplies from one of the city's fantastic markets and head to a park for an alfresco lunch.

6 Check out Atrápalo for discounted entrance tickets to popular concerts, shows and sports events in Madrid (Spanish only: www.atrapalo.com).

7 Many theatres and cinemas offer reduced ticket prices on the Día del Espectador (Viewer's Day) each week, usually a Monday, Tuesday or Wednesday.

8 Some of Madrid's bars continue the fine old tradition of providing free tapas with your drinks: these include El Tigre (Calle Infantas 23, Chueca), and La Pequeña Grañá (Calle de Embajadores 124, Embajadores).

9 Companies like SANDEMANs offer brilliant free walking tours, led by locals. Be sure to leave a tip at the end of the tour (www.neweuropetours.eu).

10 Hotel breakfasts across Spain are generally pricey and poor value: you'll eat much better elsewhere for less.

Festivals and Events

1 Carnival

A feast of colour and fun, the carnival in Madrid begins the weekend before Shrove Tuesday with music, dancing and parades. Ash Wednesday sees the "Burial of the Sardine". The mock funeral procession leaves from the church of San Antonio de la Florida and ends with the burial in the Casa de Campo, marking the start of Lent.

Carnival reveller

2 Holy Week

The celebration of the Passion of Christ is one of the most important traditions in Spain. The three days leading up to Easter see sombre but spectacular religious processions. On Holy Thursday, watch the image of Jesus being carried by penitents in traditional purple hoods and with chains around their feet. On Good Friday evening the procession of Jesús de Medinacelli leaves the basilica of the same name before winding its way around the city centre.

Grand procession on Holy Thursday

3 Patron Saints Fiestas

Madrid has two patron saints, both honoured with feast days. On 15 May the Feast of San Isidro the Labourer sees picnics, concerts and a procession to the Ermita de San Isidro. The Feast of the Virgin of Almudena takes place on 9 November when the virgin's image is paraded through the city, followed by a mass in the cathedral which bears her name (see p102).

4 Performing Arts Festivals

www.veranosdelavilla.com
■ www.madrid.org/fo

Venues all across the city host an extravaganza of dance, music, drama and film during the summer Veranos de la Villa festival and the Festival de Otoño in autumn.

5 Open-Air Classical Music

www.fundacionolivardecastillejo.org
■ www.rjb.csic.es

Enjoy a concert of classical music from mid-June to mid-September at the Fundación Olivar de Castillejo, a peaceful oasis full of olive trees in the middle of the city. Nature and classical music also come together at the Real Jardín Botánico (see pp80–81) every Friday evening in summer.

6 Art Events

www.iferma.es/arco-madrid
■ www.artemadrid.com/apertura

With one of the liveliest art scenes in Europe, Madrid hosts some major art events. ARCO art fair, usually held in February, draws artists and collectors from all over the world. In September, during Apertura Madrid, galleries and museums launch their new exhibitions with free entry over a weekend.

7 Flamenco Fever
www.madrid.org/suma
flamenca

Many of the exponents of flamenco are based in Madrid. To attend one of the most comprehensive gatherings of flamenco artists, head to the Suma Flamenca festival, usually held in June. Flamenco Madrid, hosted in spring by the Teatro Fernán Gómez (see p62), also puts on performances.

8 Fiestas del 2 Mayo
Celebrating the victory over Napoleon and the French occupation on 2 May 1808, the Day of the Community of Madrid is one of the most popular festivals in the city. Celebrations take place on Playa de Dos de Mayo, with concerts, dancing and sports competitions, followed by a military parade and fireworks.

Fiestas del 2 Mayo celebrations

9 Foodie Festivals
www.tapapies.com
■ www.gastrofestivalmadrid.com

Taste the best global cuisines at TapaPiés in October when bars and restaurants in Lavapiés offer tapas for only €3. During Gastrofestival, venues across the city stage gastronomy events in February.

10 Epiphany Celebrations
One of the most magical times during Christmas is the evening of 5 January when Madrileños celebrate Epiphany with the Procession of the Kings. Multiple floats parade through the city and the Kings throw sweets out into the crowd.

TOP 10 SPANISH CELEBRATORY CAKES

Roscón de Reyes

1 Roscón de Reyes
6 Jan
Round buns with almonds and candied fruit, usually containing a small charm.

2 Monas de Pascua
Holy Week
Very sweet brioches which are eaten with hard-boiled eggs.

3 Torrijas
Holy Week
Slices of milk-soaked bread, fried and laced with cinnamon and sugar.

4 Rosquillas del santo
15 May
Small doughnuts with a variety of flavours and bizarre names such as "the fool", "the intelligent one" and "Santa Clara".

5 Panecillos de San Antonio
13 Jun
Small rolls marked with a cross, served at the Church of San Antonio.

6 Suspiros de modistillas
13 Jun
"Needlewomen's sighs" – meringues filled with praline.

7 Buñuelos de viento
1 Nov
Small profiteroles filled with cream, custard or chocolate.

8 Huesos de santo
1 Nov
Marzipan sweets sculpted to look like "saints' bones".

9 Polvorones
Christmas
Crumbly biscuits flavoured with cinnamon and almonds.

10 Turrón
Christmas
Nougat, hard or soft, and made in various flavours.

Madrid
Area by Area

The New Castle of Manzanares el Real at the foot of the Sierra de Guadarrama mountains

TOP 10 Around Paseo del Prado

This imposing tree-lined avenue, adorned with fountains and sculptures, is home to no fewer than three world-class art galleries: the Museo Nacional Centro de Arte Reina Sofía, the Museo Nacional del Prado and the Museo Nacional Thyssen-Bornemisza. In the 18th century, the "prado" was a meadow crossed by a stream, but the rustic surroundings were deceptive, as the area had acquired an unsavoury reputation for muggings and amorous encounters. The solution, devised by Carlos IV, was a stately new boulevard between Plaza de Cibeles and Plaza de Atocha, lined with buildings devoted to the pursuit of scientific investigation. Work began in 1775 on a museum of natural history, which is now the Prado; the botanical gardens and observatory; and a medical school, which is now the Reina Sofía.

Plaza de la Lealtad

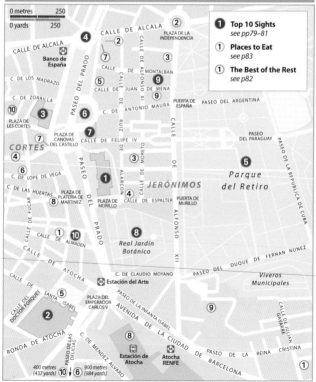

PASEO DEL PRADO

- **1** Top 10 Sights
  see pp79–81
- **1** Places to Eat
  see p83
- **1** The Best of the Rest
  see p82

The imposing façade of Palacio de Cibeles on Plaza de Cibeles

1 Museo Nacional del Prado

One of the world's finest art galleries, the Prado (see pp16–21) houses a vast collection, including Spanish paintings by Francisco Goya.

2 Museo Nacional Centro de Arte Reina Sofía

In contrast to the Prado, this gallery (see pp32–5) is devoted to the very best of 20th- and 21st-century art.

3 Museo Nacional Thyssen-Bornemisza

What began as a private collection is now a superb public museum with some of the best European art spanning the past 700 years (see pp28–31).

Museo Nacional Thyssen-Bornemisza

4 Plaza de Cibeles
MAP F4

One of Madrid's busiest traffic intersections also features the city's most famous landmark. The Cibeles Fountain was designed by Ventura Rodríguez and depicts the goddess of nature and abundance riding her chariot, pulled by a pair of prancing lions. The water-spouting cherubs were added at the end of the 19th century. The most striking architectural monument on the square is the over-the-top Palacio de Cibeles (see p50), now the Madrid Town Hall. Opposite is the Neo-Baroque Palacio de Linares, one of the city's finest 19th-century buildings, and now the Casa de América (see p63). On the corner of Calle Recoletos, partly hidden from view by its steeply sloping gardens, is the former Palacio de Buenavista. It was commissioned in 1777 for the Duchess of Alba, a legendary beauty and one-time lover of artist Francisco Goya. Today it is home to the General Army Barracks.

5 Parque del Retiro

This much-loved city park (see pp36–7) is a constant source of pleasure to Madrileños, especially on weekends and during the hot summer months. There are open spaces to enjoy, as well as wooded areas and formal gardens.

6 Plaza de la Lealtad

MAP F4 ■ Madrid Stock Exchange: Plaza de la Lealtad 1; tours by appointment: 10am Wed; email visitas@grupobme.es to book

This leafy square honours the fallen heroes of the 1808 uprising against the French *(see p47)*. The ashes of the rebel leaders, immortalized in Goya's painting *(see p17)*, were interred in the funerary urns beneath the obelisk when the project was completed in 1840. The Neo-Classical building that occupies the north side of the square is the Madrid Stock Exchange, designed by Enrique María Repullés in 1884. Visitors may admire the Corinthian-columned façade at any time, but those wishing to see the trading floor (known for its parquet flooring, painted vaults, stained-glass ceiling and gilded clock) will have to join the midday guided tour.

CIBELES VERSUS NEPTUNE

These two monuments have earned a place in city folklore and have come to symbolize the rivalry between the city's two main football clubs, Real Madrid and Atlético Madrid. When Real secures a trophy, the team and fans head for the Cibeles statue on Plaza de Cibeles *(see p79)*; when it is the turn of Atlético, Neptune **(right)**, on Plaza Canovas del Castillo, is the focus for celebrations. Both fountains have suffered damage over time so police now impose a cordon.

7 Mandarin Oriental Ritz

MAP F4 ■ Plaza de la Lealtad 5

The Ritz *(see p142)* opened in 1910 and the inauguration was attended by King Alfonso XIII, who had backed the project after complaining about the lack of quality accommodation in his capital. French architect Charles Mewes' Neo-Classical building is surprisingly understated from the outside, but the interior is opulent. Features include handwoven carpets from the Royal Tapestry factory and the *belle époque* dining room. In 2020, it was meticulously restored by the Mandarin Oriental Group.

8 Real Jardín Botánico

MAP F5 ■ Plaza de Murillo 2 ■ 914 20 30 17 ■ Open 10am–dusk daily ■ Closed 1 Jan & 25 Dec ■ Adm (free after 5pm Tue)

These gardens were inaugurated in 1781 as a centre for botanical research. Beyond the main entrance is the herbarium, with aromatic, culinary and medicinal plants. The central terrace arranges plants by family, species and genealogical

Visitors enjoying the flowers in bloom at the Real Jardín Botánico

history. Look out for an ancient tree nicknamed *"El Pantalones"*, resembling a pair of inverted trousers. More than 1,200 tropical and sub-tropical species are cultivated in the Exhibition Greenhouse, opened in 1993. The Villanueva Pavilion, which hosts art and photography exhibitions, and the arbours date from the 18th century. There is also a lovely café with a terrace and a gift shop.

9 Museo Nacional de Artes Decorativas

MAP G4 ▪ Calle de Montalbán 12 ▪ 915 32 64 99 ▪ Open 9:30am–3pm Tue–Sat, 10am–3pm Sun; Sep–Jun: 5–8pm Thu ▪ Closed 1 & 6 Jan, 1 May, 24, 25 & 31 Dec ▪ Adm (free Thu & Sat afternoons, Sun) ▪ www.culturaydeporte.gob.es/mnartesdecorativas

Housed In a 19th-century mansion overlooking the Retiro is this compelling collection of furniture, ceramics, silverware and glassware from the royal factory of La Granja, as well as jewellery, tapestries, musical instruments, clocks and toys. Arranged chronologically over four floors are reconstructed rooms illustrating Spanish domestic life from the 16th to the early 20th centuries. On the fourth floor is the recreated Valencian kitchen, decorated with over 1,600 hand-painted *azulejo* tiles. The below-stairs life of an 18th-century palace is brought to life to show servants struggling with trays of pies and desserts while the cats steal fish.

10 CaixaForum

MAP F5 ▪ Paseo del Prado 36 ▪ 913 30 73 00 ▪ Open 10am–8pm daily ▪ Closed 1 & 6 Jan, 25 Dec ▪ Adm to exhibitions (free 15 & 18 May, 9 Nov) ▪ www.caixaforum.es/madrid

It's hard to miss this cultural centre, which is set in a stunningly converted power station, crowned by a web of cast iron. Outside, there's a vertical garden, and inside are galleries for temporary exhibitions. Concerts, film screenings and talks are held here. A stylish fourth-floor café offers a close-up view of the cast-iron shell.

A DAY ON THE PASEO DEL PRADO

▶ MORNING

Begin at **Plaza de Cibeles** (see p79) and take a quick peek at the palatial central hall of the **Palacio de Cibeles** (see p50). Plans to redirect traffic away from the Paseo del Prado have been frustrated, but the central boulevard still provides a pleasant walk, with plenty of shade in summer. Follow in the footsteps of Hemingway or Dalí and enjoy a coffee at the vibrant yet relaxed atmosphere of **1912 Museo Bar** (Plaza de las Cortes 7).

Continue past the Neo-Classical façade of the **Museo Nacional del Prado** (see p79) and you'll come to **Plaza de Murillo** and the **Real Jardín Botánico**. Allow at least an hour here to make the most of the verdant tranquillity.

Upon leaving the garden, cross the Paseo del Prado and double back to **Plaza Cánovas del Castillo** and Ventura Rodríguez's splendid Neptune Fountain. The little side streets here are crammed with plenty of tempting tapas bars and restaurants. You could try **La Platería** (see p83) for a light lunch.

AFTERNOON

After lunch, take a small detour into Plaza de las Cortes, to admire the portico of the **Congreso de los Diputados** (see p82). Return to Paseo del Prado and on your left is the **Museo Nacional Thyssen-Bornemisza** (see p79) which will occupy the rest of the afternoon. Take the central boulevard to go back to **Plaza de Cibeles** (see p79), but before that head to **Estado Puro** (see p83) at Plaza Canovas del Castillo for innovative tapas.

See map on p78 ←

The Best of the Rest

Real Fábrica de Tapices

1 Real Fábrica de Tapices
MAP H6 ■ Calle Fuenterrabía 2
■ 914 34 05 50 ■ Open 10am–2pm
Mon–Fri; guided tours: 10am, 11am,
noon & 1pm; book ahead ■ Adm
■ www.realfabricadetapices.com

Artisans of the Royal Tapestry Factory
(see p59) still weave using the original
18th-century wooden looms.

2 Puerta de Alcalá
MAP G3

A Neo-Classical gateway designed
in 1769 by Francisco Sabatini.

3 Parroquia de San Jerónimo el Real
MAP F5 ■ Calle de Moreto 4
■ Open Jul–mid-Sep: 10:30am–1pm
& 6–8pm Mon, Wed & Fri; mid-Sep–
Jul: 10am–1pm & 5:30–7:30pm daily

The Castilian parliament, the Cortes,
met in this historic church in 1510.

4 Casa Museo Lope de Vega
MAP F4 ■ Calle de Cervantes,
11 ■ 914 29 92 16 ■ Open 10am–6pm
Tue–Sun (last tour 5pm) ■ www.casa
museolopedevega.org

This museum, set in Lope de Vega's
house, commemorates his life.

5 Museo Naval
MAP F4 ■ Paseo del Prado 5
■ Open 10am–7pm Tue–Sun (Aug:
to 3pm) ■ www.armada.mde.es

Among the highlights here is a
16th-century Flemish galleon and
the first map of the New World.

6 Museo del Ferrocarril
MAP F6 ■ Paseo de las Delicias
61 ■ 915 39 00 85 ■ Opening times
vary, check website ■ Adm ■ www.
museodelferrocarril.org

The railway museum has a wonderful
collection of old steam locomotives
on display and is the departure point
for the Tren de la Fresa (see p61).

7 CentroCentro
MAP F4 ■ Plaza de Cibeles 1
■ Open 10am–8pm Tue–Sun ■ Adm
■ www.centrocentro.org

Madrid's former main post office now
houses a cultural centre (see p58)
with a spectacular viewing terrace.

8 Invernadero de Atocha
MAP F6

The train station combines a sleek
modern concourse and a charming
1880s glass-and-iron construction,
now housing a lush garden (see p53).

Observatorio Astronómico's dome

9 Observatorio Astronómico
MAP G6 ■ Calle Alfonso XII 3
■ 915 06 12 61, 915 97 95 64 ■ Open
by appointment: Fri–Sun; check
website ■ Adm ■ www.ign.es

Marvel at the historic telescopes and
other astronomical instruments here.

10 Congreso de los Diputados
MAP E4 ■ Calle de Floridablanca s/n
■ 913 90 65 25 ■ Open by appointment:
noon Fri, 10:30am–12:30pm Sat (tours
in Spanish); without appointment:
noon Mon ■ www.congreso.es

Admire the Renaissance-style
sculptures and the building's portico.

Places to Eat

PRICE CATEGORIES
For a three-course meal for one with half
a bottle of wine (or equivalent meal),
taxes and extra charges.

€ under €35   €€ €35–€70   €€€ over €70

1 Matilda Café Cantina
MAP F5 ■ Calle Almadén
15 ■ 914 29 80 29 ■ Closed Mon
& Tue ■ €

This cosy place serves homemade
cakes and lunches. Enjoy the
classical music while you dine.

2 Restaurante Palacio de Cibeles
MAP F4 ■ Plaza de
Cibeles 1, 6th floor
■ 915 23 14 54 ■ €€€
Award-winning chef
Adolfo Muñoz prepares
innovative dishes using
local ingredients. The
terrace offers beautiful
views of Madrid and
the Cibeles fountain.

Restaurante Palacio de Cibeles

3 Horcher
MAP F4 ■ Calle de
Alfonso XII 6 ■ 915 22 07 31
■ Closed Sat L, Sun ■ €€€
One of Madrid's most exclusive
restaurants specializing in Central
European cuisine. Jacket required.

Luxurious interiors of Horcher

4 Restaurante Terraza El Botánico
MAP F5 ■ Calle Ruiz de Alarcón 27
■ 914 20 23 42 ■ Closed Mon ■ €
Close to the Botanical Gardens, this
elegant, family-run restaurant offers
delicious traditional Spanish cuisine.

5 Arzábal Restaurant
MAP F6 ■ Edificio Sabatini,
Museo Nacional Centre de Arte
Reina Sofía, Calle de Santa Isabel 52
■ 915 28 68 28 ■ €€

This restaurant in the Reina Sofía
museum offers fresh seasonal cuisine
and has a lovely outdoor terrace.

6 Los Gatos
MAP E5 ■ Calle de Jesús 2
■ 914 29 30 67 ■ Closed Mon ■ €
With quirky decor, this unique tapas
bar (see p66) is a cool place for quick
bites and beers.

7 Estado Puro
MAP F5 ■ Plaza
Cánovas del Castillo 4
■ 917 79 30 36 ■ €€
Indulge in an early
lunch on the terrace of
this restaurant (see p69)
set close to the Prado
and Thyssen museum.
On offer are innovative
tapas and local wines.

8 La Platería
MAP F5 ■ Moratín 49
■ 914 29 17 22 ■ €
Situated off the Paseo del Prado,
there's a terrace where you can
snack on Castilian dishes such as
jamón Ibérico and goat's cheese
while you watch the world go by.

9 Viridiana
MAP F4 ■ Calle Juan de
Mena 14 ■ 915 31 10 39 ■ Closed
Sun D ■ €€€
Master chef Abraham García's bistro
offers a menu of traditional Spanish
dishes and a great wine list (see p68).

10 Bodegas Rosell
MAP F6 ■ Calle General
Lacy 14 ■ 914 67 84 58 ■ Closed Mon,
Aug ■ www.bodegasrosell.es ■ €
This classic Madrid tavern (see
p67) serves great value wines and
generous portions of splendid tapas.
Booking is recommended.

See map on p78

TOP 10 Salamanca and Recoletos

Museo de Escultura al Aire Libre

One of Madrid's most affluent neighbourhoods, Salamanca is named after its founder, José de Salamanca y Mayol (1811–83). The Marquis first saw the commercial possibilities of the area in the 1860s and transformed it with grid-patterned streets and elegant mansions. The new neighbourhood was an immediate hit with the upper classes who found the central districts stifling, and their antiquated homes lacking in amenities such as flushing toilets and hot running water. Salamanca soon acquired a reputation as a bastion of conservatism and its residents were among the most loyal supporters of the Franco regime. Today the streets around Calle de Serrano, Calle de Goya and Calle de Velázquez form Madrid's premier shopping district.

① Café Gijón
MAP F3 ▪ Paseo de Recoletos 21 ▪ 915 21 54 25, 915 31 03 18 ▪ www.cafegijon.com ▪ €€

The haunt of journalists and leading cultural figures, the Gijón was founded in 1888 and is one of the few surviving *tertulia* (literary) cafés where, traditionally, men gathered to discuss issues of the day. Former patrons include the poet Federico García Lorca, the American film director Orson Welles and, more improbably, the famous Dutch spy Mata Hari. Order tapas and drinks at the bar or book a table for lunch. The café also has a pleasant terrace.

② Museo Arqueológico Nacional

The scale of the Archaeological Museum's collections *(see pp38–9)* can be daunting, so home in on what interests you most. The star turn on the main floor is the *Lady of Elche*, a stone bust of an Iberian noblewoman

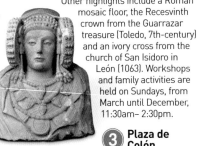

Lady of Elche

from the 4th century BC. There is a niche in the back to hold the ashes of the dead, which is typical of the funerary rites of Iberian culture.

Other highlights include a Roman mosaic floor, the Recesvinth crown from the Guarrazar treasure (Toledo, 7th-century) and an ivory cross from the church of San Isidoro in León (1063). Workshops and family activities are held on Sundays, from March until December, 11:30am– 2:30pm.

③ Plaza de Colón
MAP F2

Named after Christopher Columbus, this expansive square contains three monumental slabs near Calle de Serrano, symbolizing the ships that made the voyage to America in 1492. There is also a conventional 19th-century sculpture of Columbus. The base shows Queen Isabella I of Castile selling her jewellery to finance the trip. Throughout history, the square has been used as a place for demonstrations.

For a key to restaurant price ranges see p91

④ Museo Lázaro Galdiano
MAP G1 ■ Calle de Serrano 122
■ Metro Rubén Darío or Gregorio
Marañón ■ Open 9:30am–3pm Tue–
Sat, 10am–3pm Sun ■ Closed Mon &
public hols ■ Adm (free 2–3pm)

José Lázaro Galdiano (1862–1947)
was a patron of the arts and a
passionate collector whose Italian-
style palazzo is now a museum
showcasing his fabulous possessions. On display here are Spanish
works by El Greco, Velázquez and
Goya, and European paintings by
Constable and Gainsborough. You'll
find spectacular *objets d'art*, too.

***Adoration of the Magi* by El Greco**

SALAMANCA AND RECOLETOS

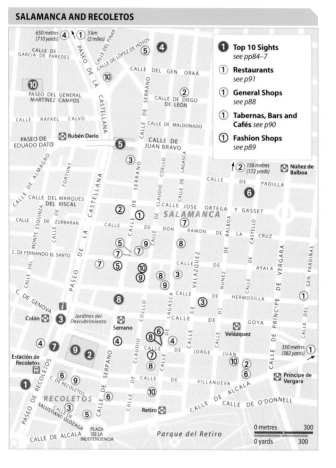

	Top 10 Sights see pp84–7
1	Restaurants see p91
1	General Shops see p88
1	Tabernas, Bars and Cafés see p90
1	Fashion Shops see p89

5 Museo de Escultura al Aire Libre

MAP G1 ▪ Paseo de la Castellana 40

Situated beneath a road bridge, the open-air sculpture museum is easily overlooked. Nevertheless, exhibited in its windswept precincts are works by a number of outstanding modern Spanish sculptors, including Eduardo Chillida, Julio González, Joan Miró and Pablo Serrano.

6 Fundación Juan March

MAP H1 ▪ Castelló 77

One of Spain's most vital cultural institutions was founded in 1955 by the banker Juan March Ordinas, to promote contemporary Spanish art. Madrid shares the permanent collection (especially strong on abstract artists of the 1950s such as Tàpies, Sempere, Saura and Millares) with other branches of the foundation in Cuenca and Palma de Mallorca, but the foundation's (see p63) main attractions are its outstanding temporary exhibitions.

7 Paseo de Recoletos

MAP F3

"Paseo" implies a stroll and this lovely avenue, at its best on a sunny morning or just after sun-set, was designed precisely for that purpose. The first cafés in this area began to appear in the 19th century when the boulevard was nicknamed "Recoletos beach". Most of the originals had disappeared by the 1980s when the Movida gave the terraces a new lease of life. The Pabellón de Espejo looks the part with its

A café at Paseo de Recoletos

painted tiles and wrought-iron adornments but actually dates from the 1990s. No. 10 was the residence of the Marqués de Salamanca.

Visitors at the plush Calle de Serrano

8 Calle de Serrano

MAP G3

Running through the heart of the Salamanca district is Madrid's smartest shopping street. Here, top Spanish designer names such as Loewe, Purificación García and Roberto Verino rub shoulders with Armani, Gucci, Yves Saint Laurent and Cartier. Even if you're not especially interested in fashion, there's plenty to amuse you. Madrid's best-known department store, El Corte Inglés, has branches at Nos. 47 and 52, while Agatha Ruíz de la Prada is at No. 27. If you're looking for gifts, visit Adolfo Dominguez's concept store (No. 5), which stocks great gifts, jewellery and accessories. For a bite to eat, head to the Corte Inglés (No. 52) and choose from one of their restaurants in the Gourmet Experience (6th & 7th floors).

9 Biblioteca Nacional

MAP F3 ▪ Paseo de Recoletos
20–22 ▪ Library: open 9am–9pm
Mon–Fri; museum: open 10am–8pm
Mon–Sat (to 2pm Sun & public hols)

Founded in 1712 by Felipe V, Spain's
National Library is one of the world's
largest. It has occupied its current
home, an immense Neo-Classical
building on Paseo de Recoletos,
since the end of the 19th century.
Highlights of its collection include
26 rare 17th-century editions of
Cervantes' classic, *Don Quixote*,
and drawings and etchings by illus-
trious artists from Goya to Velázquez.
The reading rooms are open only to
holders of a reader's card, but the
exhibition galleries and fascinating
museum are open to all.

10 Museo Sorolla

MAP F1 ▪ Paseo del General
Martínez Campos 37 ▪ Open
9:30am–8pm Tue–Sat, 10am–3pm
Sun & public hols ▪ Closed Mon &
some public hols ▪ Adm

This museum *(see p49)* is devoted
to the Valencian artist Joaquín
Sorolla y Bastida (1863–1923) who
spent the last 13 years of his life
here. Some rooms have been left
as they were in his lifetime, while
others are used to hang his work.
Dubbed "the Spanish Impressionist",
his subject matter varies hugely,
but Sorolla is at his most appealing
when evoking the sea. Don't leave
without seeing the Andalucían-
style garden.

The Bathing of the Horse (1909)
by Joaquín Sorolla y Bastida

See map on p85 ←

A DAY'S SHOPPING

▶ MORNING

Leave **Serrano Metro Station**,
heading south and limber up with
a spot of window shopping on
Salamanca's main fashion drag.
Turn left into Calle Columela –
try not to pay too much attention
to **Pastelería Mallorca's** mouth-
watering displays of cakes and
pastries *(see p88)*. Then turn left
into Calle Claudio Coello, which
is lined with antique shops and
boutiques. Don't miss Galería
Fernando Pradilla (No. 20),
Cristina Castañer (No. 51) and
stylish concept store **Isolée** (No.
55) *(see p89)*. Cross Calle de Goya,
then continue along **Calle de
Claudio Coello** and head to **Calle
de Hermosilla**. Finish at Centro
Comercial ABC Serrano, which
has great views and is excellent
to enjoy a drink and meal.

Many shops take a long lunch
break so this is the perfect time
to stop for lunch. Choices abound,
but leading contenders include
El Pimiento Verde - Lagasca *(see
p90)*, which offers superb Basque
fare, the tapas bar at **Restaurante
O'Caldiño** *(see p90)* or **Restaurante
La Maruca** *(Calle de Velázquez, 54)*
for a wide variety of Spanish food.

AFTERNOON

When you're ready, head south
towards the vibrant thoroughfare
of **Calle de Jorge Juan**, which
has a number of designer shops,
such as **Pedro Garcia** and **Paule
Ka**. Return to Calle de Serrano,
Madrid's boutique boulevard,
where you can either ogle over
the designer goods and dream,
or blow your budget on a beautiful handbag or a pair of shoes.

General Shops

El Corte Inglés

1 El Corte Inglés
MAP H2 ■ Calle de Goya 76

This branch of Madrid's best-known department store also has a beauty parlour, restaurant and supermarket, as well as the usual departments.

2 L.A. Studio
MAP H3 ■ Calle de Castelló 8
■ www.lastudio.es

Rifle through an amazing range of antiques and *objets d'art,* from retro sofas and Art Deco lamps, to original oil paintings and gilded glasses.

3 Centro Comercial ABC Serrano
MAP G1 ■ Calle de Serrano 61

Salamanca's other main shopping centre also has a good selection of boutiques (including a branch of the Spanish chain of children's clothing, Neck & Neck).

4 Centro de Anticuarios Lagasca
MAP G3 ■ Calle de Lagasca 36

Antiques-lovers can save time exploring individual shops by visiting this gallery, which brings together Madrid's reputable dealers.

5 Bombonería Santa
MAP G1 ■ Calle de Serrano 56

If you love chocolate, look no further than this tiny outlet on Serrano which also sells gift-wrapped sweets. The speciality here is *leña vieja* (chocolates that are cast to resemble tree trunks).

6 Pastelería Mallorca
MAP G3 ■ Calle de Serrano 6
■ Open 9am–9pm daily

A reputable delicatessen chain, Pastelería Mallorca offers a mouth-watering selection of cheese, ham, pastries, cakes and ice cream. Stock up for a picnic, or visit the bar.

7 Frutas Vázquez
MAP G2 ■ Calle de Ayala 11

This small, but famous family-run fruit vendor includes, it is said, Queen Sofía among its patrons. The selection of tropical fruits will stir the taste buds.

8 Mercado de la Paz
MAP G2 ■ Calle de Ayala 28
■ Open 9am–8pm Mon–Fri (to 2:30pm Sat)

Salamanca's best-known food market (*see p71*) is worth tracking down for its Spanish delicacies, as well as for its surprisingly wide range of international cheese.

Vibrant market, Mercado de la Paz

9 Delivinos Urban Gourmet
MAP G2 ■ Calle Cid 2 ■ Open 10am–10pm Mon–Sat, 11am–6pm Sun

Specialising in premium wine and liqueurs, this delicatessen also offers luxury gourmet products such as cheeses, olives and charcuterie.

10 Aneko
MAP H3 ■ Calle Castelló 15

This delightful shop stocks an array of beautiful Japanese products, including colourful kimonos, bags, gifts and handmade tableware such as saké glasses.

Fashion Shops

1 Villalba
MAP G2 ■ Calle de Serrano 68

Spanish celebrities love Alfredo Villalba's luxurious and highly original designs for women, and his dresses, often elaborately beaded, have adorned many a red carpet.

2 Isabel Marant Madrid
MAP F2 ■ Calle de Jorge Juan 12

An esteemed fashion store offering designs of excellent quality for both women and men. You can find another nearby branch at Serrano 47.

3 NAC
MAP H2 ■ Calle de Hermosilla 34

A favourite with Madrid's fashion connoisseurs, NAC selects designs from more than 50 labels to create a chic, urban yet relaxed look.

4 Loewe
MAP G2 ■ Calle de Serrano 34

Loewe may not sound Spanish, but is in fact one of Spain's longest established names – the first Madrid shop opened in 1846. Renowned for accessories, especially leather.

Interior at Loewe

5 Roberto Verino
MAP G2 ■ Calle de Serrano 33

Men's and women's fashions and accessories by another of Spain's flagship designers. Claims to cater to confident women who know what they want to wear.

6 Pretty Ballerinas
MAP G3 ■ Calle de Lagasca 30

A handmade shoe shop specializing in ballerina shoes and other flat women's shoes, Pretty Ballerinas is a family business with a history dating back to 1918. Each pair of shoes sold here is delicately made on the island of Madeira.

7 Circo Kids'.
MAP G3 ■ Calle Jorge Juan 14

This store offers beautiful clothes and toys for young children, inspired by simple and sustainable designs. Look out for the popular Made in Spain collection.

8 Marcos Luengo
MAP G3 ■ Calle de Jorge Juan 16

Head to Marcos Luengo's store to discover his diverse collections. Look out for the leather handbags which are his hallmark.

9 Cristina Castañer
MAP G3 ■ Calle de Claudio Coello 51

Espadrilles are not generally associated with high fashion, but this Spanish designer has turned them into an art form. All colours and styles from casual to evening wear are on offer.

10 Isolée
MAP G3 ■ Calle de Claudio Coello 55

One of Madrid's first concept stores, Isolée mixes fashion, design and gourmet food under one roof. It's ultra-hip, from its sleek café to its cool choice of music.

See map on p85

Tabernas, Bars and Cafés

1 **Taberna de la Daniela**

Calle de General Pardiñas 21 ▪ Metro Goya ▪ 915 75 23 29 ▪ €€

Embellished with *azulejos*, this traditional *taberna* (see p51) is known for its *Cocido Madrileño* (Madrid stew) that is prepared using fresh ingredients.

2 **Tasca La Farmacia**

MAP G1 ▪ Calle de Diego de León 9 ▪ 915 64 86 52 ▪ Open L & D ▪ €

This former pharmacy (see p66) has attractive *azulejo* decoration. It specializes in variants of *bacalao* (cod).

3 **a.n.E.l Tapas Bar & Lounge**

MAP F3 ▪ Calle Villalar 1 ▪ 914 35 51 06 ▪ €

Great selection of reasonably priced tapas, and regional mains. Unwind with a glass of wine on the terrace.

4 **El Espejo**

MAP F3 ▪ Paseo de Recoletos 31 ▪ 913 08 23 47 ▪ Closed 24 Dec ▪ €

Choose between the main restaurant or the elegant terrace and conservatory. The terrace serves only a set menu or tapas and a pianist will serenade you during the summer.

Taberna de la Daniela

5 **Cervecería José Luis**

MAP G2 ▪ Calle de Serrano 89 ▪ 915 63 09 58 ▪ €€

Attracting a loyal local clientele, the tapas here are said to be among the best in the city. The tortilla is heavenly.

6 **El Perro y la Galleta**

MAP H3 ▪ Calle de Castelló 12 ▪ 610 18 17 11 ▪ €€

Close to Parque del Retiro (see pp36–7), this restaurant serves creative tapas and tasty mains in a cosy atmosphere.

7 **Restaurante O'Caldiño**

MAP H2 ▪ Calle de Lagasca 74 ▪ 915 75 70 14 ▪ €€

A cosy and classic tavern with seasonal Galician dishes, Restaurante O'Caldiño has a particular focus on seafood.

8 **O'Caldiño**

MAP G2 ▪ Calle Lagasca 74 ▪ 915 75 70 14 ▪ Closed 1 Jan, 24, 25 & 31 Dec ▪ €€

Offering Galician cuisine, this elegant tapas bar has been serving excellent seafood since 1973.

9 **El Pimiento Verde**

MAP G2 ▪ Calle de Lagasca 43 ▪ 910 74 14 54 ▪ €€

Famous for its artichoke dishes, this Basque-style *taberna* also serves cod, monkfish and steaks, along with Spanish wines.

10 **Pinchos Elcano**

Calle Lagasca 7 ▪ 911 27 25 24 ▪ €

This rustic bar situated in the heart of the Salamanca area, specializes in delicious sandwiches, burgers and exquisite traditional basque-style tapas known as *pinchos*.

The terrace at El Espejo

Restaurants

PRICE CATEGORIES
For a three-course meal for one with half a bottle of wine (or equivalent meal), taxes and extra charges.
....
€ under €35   €€ €35–€70   €€€ over €70

DiverXO
Calle de Padre Damián 23 ▪ 915 70 07 66 ▪ Metro Cuzco ▪ Closed Mon ▪ €€€

Indulge in an avant-garde gastronomic journey at this three-starred Michelin restaurant *(see p68)*. No vegetarian or vegan options available. Book in advance.

② St James Juan Bravo
MAP H1 ▪ Calle de Juan Bravo 26 ▪ 915 75 60 10 ▪ €€€

A fantastic seafood restaurant, St James Juan Bravo has an extensive menu, though many come for the famous paella.

③ Restorante La Trainera
MAP G3 ▪ Calle de Lagasca 60 ▪ 915 76 80 35 ▪ Closed Sun, Aug ▪ €€€

Renowned for its seafood, this dainty restaurant has a well thought-out Spanish wine selection to complement the daily catches.

④ Leña Madrid. Las Brasas x Dani García
MAP F1 ▪ Hotel Hyatt Regency Hesperia, P. de la Castellana 57 ▪ 911 08 55 66 ▪ €€€

One of Madrid's greatest fine dining restaurants, by famous chef Dani García. Do not miss the burgers and the "Tarta di Rose".

⑤ Restaurante Ramses.Life
MAP G3 ▪ Plaza de la Independencia 4 ▪ 914 35 16 66 ▪ €€

This super-stylish restaurant *(see p65)* serves an eclectic mix of international dishes. Alfresco dining is available throughout the year.

⑥ Al-Mounia
MAP G3 ▪ Calle de Recoletos 5 ▪ 914 35 08 28 ▪ €€

Specializing in North African cuisine, this Moroccan restaurant offers tasty dishes made from traditional recipes passed over generations.

⑦ Ten con Ten
MAP G2 ▪ Calle Ayala 6 ▪ 915 75 92 54 ▪ Closed Sun, public hols ▪ €€

This stylish restaurant has several beautifully decorated dining rooms. Meticulously prepared dishes include beef with truffled mashed potatoes.

⑧ Sottosopra
MAP G3 ▪ Calle de Puigcerd 8 ▪ 917 48 61 97 ▪ €€

Tuck into delicious Italian food on Sottosopra's lovely outdoor terrace, which sits in a quiet alley.

Chic interiors of Ramón Freixa Madrid

⑨ Ramón Freixa Madrid
MAP G3 ▪ Calle Claudio Coello 67 ▪ 917 81 82 62 ▪ Closed Mon, Tue & Sun D, Easter, Aug, Christmas ▪ €€€

Star chef Ramón Freixa's gastronomic mecca *(see p69)* received its second Michelin star in 2010.

⑩ BiBo Andalusian Brasserie & Tapas
MAP G1 ▪ Paseo de la Castellana 52 ▪ 918 05 25 56 ▪ €€

The menu here offers Andalusian cuisine and an extensive wine list.

See map on p85

🔟 Downtown Madrid

Central Madrid began to take on its present appearance in the mid-19th century with the modernisation of Puerta del Sol. This busy intersection was the first to have electric street lighting, trams and, in 1919, Madrid's first metro station. Meanwhile Calle de Alcalá was becoming the focal point of a new financial district as banks and other businesses set up their headquarters in showy new premises. Building work on the Gran Vía began in 1910 but was only completed in the 1940s with the remodelling of Plaza de España. To make way for this sweeping Parisian-style boulevard, 1,315 m (1,440 yds) long and designed with automobile traffic in mind, more than 300 buildings were demolished and 14 streets disappeared. The new avenue reflected the American architectural tastes of the jazz age, with skyscrapers, cinemas, glitzy cocktail bars, luxury hotels, theatres and restaurants.

Bear climbing an arbutus tree, the symbol of the city

DOWNTOWN MADRID

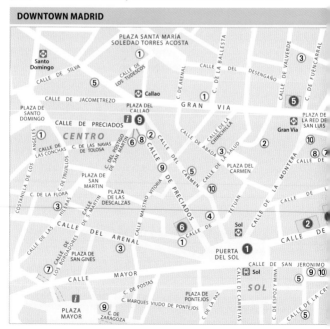

① Puerta del Sol
MAP N4

Ten streets radiate from this buzzing, oval-shaped square, which for most *Madrileños* is the real heart of the city. The name actually means "Gateway of the Sun" although the gateway itself was demolished in 1570. Of numerous historic events to take place here, the most dramatic occurred during the 1808 insurrection when snipers fired on one of Napoleon's soldiers, provoking a massacre. Dominating the square's south side is the 18th-century Casa de Correos, a post office which later became the Ministry of the Interior, and now houses the regional government. A marker in front of the building indicates *"kilómetro cero"*, from which all distances in Spain are calculated. In the square's centre is a statue of Carlos III and, on the corner of Calle del Carmen, is a bronze statue of a bear climbing an arbutus tree (*madroño* in Spanish) – the symbol of the city.

② Real Casa de la Aduana
MAP P4 ■ Calle de Alcalá 5, 7, 9 & 11 ■ Closed to the public

The royal customs house was a cornerstone of Carlos III's plans to improve the appearance of the city. In 1761, the queen's stables and 16 houses were demolished to make way for Francisco Sabatini's Neo-Classical masterpiece. Enormous amounts of money were lavished on the façade alone, the decorative features of which include ashlar columns and a balcony bearing the royal coat of arms. It is now the head-quarters of the Ministry of Economy and Finance.

Real Casa de la Aduana

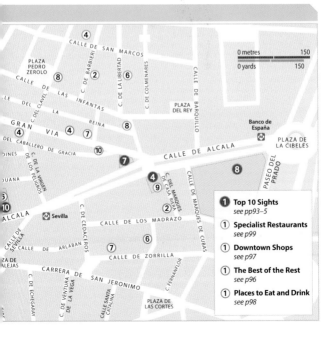

PLAZA PEDRO ZEROLO

CALLE DE SAN MARCOS

C. DE BARBIERI

C. DE LA LIBERTAD

C. DE COLMENARES

CALLE DE BARQUILLO

PLAZA DEL REY

CALLE DE LAS INFANTAS

CALLE DEL CLAVEL

GRAN VIA

REINA

DEL CABALLERO DE GRACIA

C. DE LA VIRGEN DE LOS PELIGROS

Banco de España

PLAZA DE LA CIBELES

CALLE DE ALCALA

PASEO DEL PRADO

C. DEL MARQUES DE CASA RIERA

CALLE DE MARQUES DE CUBAS

Sevilla

C. DE CEDACEROS

CALLE DE LOS MADRAZO

CALLE DE ARLABAN

CALLE DE ZORRILLA

CARRERA DE SAN JERONIMO

C. DE VENTURA DE LA VEGA

CALLE SANTA CATALINA

C. FERNANFLOR

PLAZA DE LAS CORTES

C. DE ECHEGARAY

0 metres 150
0 yards 150

① **Top 10 Sights**
see pp93–5

① **Specialist Restaurants**
see p99

① **Downtown Shops**
see p97

① **The Best of the Rest**
see p96

① **Places to Eat and Drink**
see p98

③ Real Academia de Bellas Artes de San Fernando

MAP P3 ▪ Calle de Alcalá 13 ▪ Open 10am–3pm Tue–Sun & public hols ▪ Closed Mon ▪ Adm

Founded in the 18th century, the palatial Academy of Fine Arts houses a collection of paintings surpassed only by the Prado and the Thyssen-Bornemisza. Outstanding among the Spanish paintings are the Goyas, including the classic fiesta scene, *Burial of the Sardine*. There are also impressive works by European masters including Bellini, Tintoretto, Van Dyck, Rubens and Titian. Picasso and Dalí studied here for a time.

The lively Círculo de Bellas Artes

④ Círculo de Bellas Artes

MAP R3 ▪ Calle Alcalá 42 ▪ Open 9am–7pm Mon–Thu (to 5pm Fri); exhibitions: 11am–2pm & 5–9pm Tue–Sun ▪ Closed 1 Jan, 24, 25 & 31 Dec ▪ Exhibitions closed in Aug ▪ Adm

While the golden age of the Fine Arts Club occurred in the 1920s and 1930s, this organization is still thriving today. The Círculo promotes Spanish and world culture, with theatre and ballet productions, exhibitions, art films, workshops and conferences. It even has a magazine and a radio station.

ERNEST HEMINGWAY

The famous American writer Ernest Hemingway arrived in Madrid in March 1937 to find a city under siege. He stayed in the Hotel Florida (since demolished) on Plaza del Callao, and recalled dodging shells and bullets on Gran Vía as he made his way to the Telefónica building to file his stories.

---

⑤ Edificio Telefónica

MAP P2 ▪ Gran Vía 28 ▪ Open 10am–8pm Tue–Sun ▪ Closed Mon, 1 & 6 Jan, 25 Dec, public hols

Now headquarters of Spain's national telephone company, this was Madrid's first high-rise building. Designed by American architect Lewis Weeks and constructed by Ignacio de Cárdenas in 1929, it reflects the values of the Chicago School, then much in vogue. The Telefónica building played an important role in the Civil War when it was used by the Republican army to observe enemy troop movements in the Casa de Campo. Franco's forces found it an ideal range finder for their artillery. The Fundación de Arte y Tecnología Telefónica has an exhibition on the history of communications as well as a splendid art collection, with works by Picasso, Juan Gris and Antoni Tàpies. Another room on the ground floor hosts temporary exhibitions.

⑥ El Corte Inglés

MAP N3 ▪ Calle de Preciados 3

The story of the founder of Spain's premier department store, Ramón Areces Rodríguez, is a classic tale of rags-to-riches. At the age of 15, Areces emigrated to Cuba and worked as a shop assistant before returning to Spain in 1934. The following year he opened a small tailor's in Calle de Preciados and never looked back. It's hard to miss the distinctive white shopping bags with the green logo. There are numerous branches in the capital.

⑦ Edificio Metrópolis

MAP R3 ▪ Corner Gran Vía & Calle de Alcalá

The original owners of this landmark *(see p50)*, La Unión y el Fénix insurance company, commissioned the striking statue on the cupola. Known as *"Ave Fenix"*, it represents the fabled bird that died on a funeral pyre but rose from the flames once every 500 years. When the Metrópolis company moved into the building, it inherited the sculpture, which then lost its significance.

Façade of Banco de España

⑧ Banco de España
MAP F4 ■ Calle de Alcalá 48

The Bank of Spain was founded in 1856, and 20 years later acquired the exclusive right to issue bank notes in its name. The most impressive part of these headquarters is the corner section, decorated with typical Neo-Baroque ornamentation, a marble clock and the distinctive golden globe. Spain's gold reserves are locked away in the vaults beneath Plaza de Cibeles (see p79). Apart from gold, the bank's main treasure is its art collection, with works ranging from Goya to Tàpies. It can be viewed only by written application to the bank.

⑨ Plaza del Callao
MAP M2

This square reflects the modernist architecture of 1930s America. Good examples are the Edificio Cine Callao (No. 3), the Palacio de la Prensa (No. 4), the former headquarters of the Press Association, and the Palacio de la Música (Gran Vía 35), which today houses both the Cine Capitol cinema (see p96) and the Hotel Vincci Capitol (Gran Vía 41).

⑩ Casino de Madrid
MAP Q3 ■ Calle de Alcalá 15

This exclusive gentlemen's club was founded in 1910. The florid architecture is typical of the period, but the lavish interior is rarely open to the public. Non-members are allowed in the restaurant, La Terraza Del Casino, which has two Michelin stars.

Casino de Madrid

A DAY'S STROLL AROUND DOWNTOWN MADRID

▶ MORNING

Start the walk outside the Casa de Correos in **Puerta del Sol** (see p93), a popular meeting point for Madrileños. Cross the square in the direction of the bus stops, then turn on to Calle de Alcalá. This busy street is lined with fine examples of 18th- and 19th-century architecture. Two examples on your left are the **Real Casa de la Aduana** and the **Real Academia de Bellas Artes de San Fernando**. Take time to visit this often overlooked gallery, with its small, but quality, collection of paintings. Next door is the showy façade of the **Casino de Madrid**.

Cross **Calle de Alcalá** when you reach the junction with **Gran Vía** (see p73), then head for coffee in the **Círculo de Bellas Artes**. As you make your way back to Gran Vía, look up to admire the **Edificio Metrópolis** building, then take a stroll along Madrid's bustling main avenue.

For lunch, escape the crowds by turning into Calle de Hortaleza, then Calle Reina. At No. 29 is **La Barraca**, famous for its paellas.

AFTERNOON

Head back to **Gran Vía** and (see p73) continue to **Plaza del Callao**. Turn left into **Calle de Preciados**, a pedestrianized street that is dominated by its two large department stores, **FNAC** (see p97) and **El Corte Inglés** (see p94).

After a leisurely browse around the shops, return to Puerta del Sol as it begins to liven up for the evening.

See map on pp92–3

The Best of the Rest

Café Berlin
MAP L3 ■ Costanilla de los Ángeles 20 ■ Closed Mon

This is one of Madrid's best venues for live music, with an eclectic programme which features everything from salsa and reggae to jazz and flamenco. Concerts are followed by DJ sessions.

2 Cine Estudio Círculo de Bellas Artes
MAP E4 ■ Calle Marqués de la Casa Riera 4 ■ Closed Aug

The cinema of the fine arts centre (see p94) shows classic movies by 20th-century directors such as Eisenstein, Fassbinder, Francis Ford Coppola and John Huston.

3 Palacio de Gaviria
MAP D4 ■ Calle del Arenal, 9

With Palazzo-style architecture, this 19th-century gem served as a nightclub between 1991 and 2011. After renovation, it reopened in 2017 as a venue for Arthemisia, an Italian company known for hosting temporary and permanent art exhibitions.

4 Centro del Ejército y la Armada (Casino Militar)
MAP Q3 ■ Gran Vía 13

Inaugurated in 1916, this building has Modernista twirls and is home to a military cultural association. Its salons host concerts and dances.

5 Cine Capitol
MAP M2 ■ Gran Vía 41

Located in the Art Deco Carrión building, this cinema's greatest moment occurred early in the Civil War when Eisenstein's stirring movie *Kronstadt* was shown to an audience that included the President of the Republic and leading military figures. Films are screened in Spanish. There are three screens that include digital 3D technology.

6 Teatro de la Zarzuela
MAP R4 ■ Calle de Jovellanos 4

Built to showcase Spain's unique light opera form, *Zarzuela*, this theatre (see p62) also hosts international opera, music recitals and other events.

7 Museo ICO
MAP P3 ■ Calle de Zorrilla 3 ■ Closed Mon

A modern gallery, Museo ICO hosts exhibitions focused on Spanish architecture and urban planning. It also offers guided tours and workshops.

8 Sala El Sol
MAP P3 ■ Calle de los Jardines 3 ■ Closed Sun & Mon

A venue for concerts by Spanish and international bands, Sala El Sol dates from the Movida period of cultural change in the late 1970s.

9 Calle Preciados
MAP N3–N4

One of the most popular shopping streets in central Madrid, this pedestrianized artery is home to El Corte Inglés, FNAC and Zara.

10 Iglesia de Nuestra Señora del Carmen
MAP N3 ■ Calle Carmen 10

This 17th-century church contains a venerated statue of the Virgin, which is paraded around the city on the saint's feast day (16 July), and a rather gory, but equally revered, Baroque statue of the Recumbent Christ.

Interiors of Nuestra Señora del Carmen

Downtown Shops

 Zara
MAP N2 ■ Gran Vía 34

Known as a Spanish fashion phenomenon, Zara is now also a household name throughout Europe and the United States. Stylish clothes for all the family at reasonable prices.

Shopfront of FNAC

② FNAC
MAP N3 ■ Calle de Preciados 28

A useful store, just a few minutes' walk from Puerta del Sol, sells everything from CDs and sound systems to cameras, DVDs, books and mobile phones. There are helpful floor staff, some of whom speak a little English.

③ El Horno de San Onofre
MAP P2 ■ Calle de S Onofre 3

The decor of this traditional Madrid bakery borders on the palatial. The products are just as good – every type of bread, as well as seasonal specialities such as *roscón de Reyes (see p75)* and *turrón* (Christmas nougat).

④ Real Madrid Official Store
MAP N4 ■ Calle Carmen 3

A place of pilgrimage for Real Madrid's army of fans, Los Blancos (The Whites), this shop sells football strips, footballs and souvenirs.

⑤ o2 Lifestyle Zone
MAP N3 ■ Calle del Carmen 16

Raid this store near Puerta del Sol for glitzy costume jewellery and equally showy accessories. Head for the first floor for imaginative gift ideas.

⑥ La Central de Callao Bookshop
MAP C3 ■ Calle del Postigo de San Martín 8

This bookshop and cultural centre stretches over three floors, with a café-restaurant (El Bistró) and a cocktail bar (El Garito) as well as an array of cultural activities.

⑦ Loewe
MAP E4 ■ Gran Vía 8

If you are a fan of the Spanish brand Loewe, then head to Gran Vía 8. This is the original store that opened in 1939. Check out its guestbook whose signatories include Grace Kelly.

⑧ Desigual
MAP M3 ■ Calle de Preciados 25

Quirky Spanish clothing brand, specializing in colourful styles for men, women and children, as well as home accessories.

Façade of Antigua Relojería

⑨ Antigua Relojería
MAP M4 ■ Calle La Sal 2

Established in 1880, this inviting shop specializes in watches. Its interior still has original 1930s wooden cabinets and drawers, and there's a clock featuring a jolly watch-maker outside.

⑩ Grassy
MAP R3 ■ Gran Vía 1

This famous jeweller occupies one of the signature buildings of the Gran Vía dating from 1916. The gleaming window displays of rings, watches and other items (all original designs) are equally distinguished.

See map on pp92–3

Places to Eat and Drink

1 Casa Labra
MAP N4 ▪ Calle de Tetuán 12 ▪ 915 31 00 81 ▪ Closed Sun & 1–28 Aug ▪ €

This pub *(see p67)* was where Pablo Iglesias founded the Spanish Workers' Party in 1879. Be sure to try the *soldaditos de pavía* (fried cod).

Tapas at Fatigas del Querer

2 Artemisa Vegetarian Restaurant
MAP P3 ▪ Calle de las Tres Cruces 4 ▪ 915 21 87 21 ▪ €

An exclusively vegan and gluten-free restaurant, it offers delectable, imaginative dishes, along with organic wines and soothing herbal teas.

3 El Escarpín
MAP M3 ▪ Calle de las Hileras 17 ▪ 915 59 99 57 ▪ €

A fine Asturian tavern renowned for serving regional specialities such as *fabada* (bean stew) and *chorizo a la sidra* (sausage stew in cider).

4 Museo Chicote
MAP Q3 ▪ Gran Vía 12 ▪ 915 32 67 37 ▪ €€

Ernest Hemingway put this cocktail bar *(see p64)* on the map in the 1930s; other famous visitors included Frank Sinatra and Orson Welles.

5 Fatigas del Querer
MAP P4 ▪ Calle de la Cruz 17 ▪ 915 23 21 31 ▪ €

There is a wide range of tapas on offer in this quaint Andalucían tavern *(see p51)*. Try the *raciones*, Iberian ham, seafood and fresh fried fish. It is always lively here, especially at night.

6 La Terraza del Casino
MAP Q3 ▪ Calle Alcalá 15 ▪ 915 32 12 75 ▪ Closed Sun, Mon & public hols ▪ €€€

Madrid's historic casino's Michelin-starred restaurant is run by Chef Paco Roncero. It features a terrace with panoramic views, and some of the finest cuisine in Spain. Formal attire is required and children under the age of 12 are not allowed.

7 Yerbabuena
MAP M4 ▪ Calle de Bordadores 3 ▪ 915 99 48 05 ▪ Closed Sun D ▪ €

This bright, cheery café offers vegan, vegetarian, and coeliac-suitable fare. Complete your meal with one of their delicious homemade desserts.

8 La Terraza de Óscar
MAP E3 ▪ Hotel Room Mate Óscar, Plaza de Pedro Zerolo 12 ▪ 917 01 10 69 ▪ €€

A cocktail bar offering excellent views over Madrid's skyline.

9 Museo del Jamón
MAP P4 ▪ Carrera de San Jerónimo 6 ▪ 915 21 03 46 ▪ €

Snack on delicious cold cuts, cheeses, cakes and sandwiches at this restaurant and delicatessen.

10 Priorité Art Coffee Shop
MAP R3 ▪ Calle de la Montera 42 ▪ 915 31 40 37 ▪ €

A friendly, arty, simple café, where you can enjoy inexpensive drinks and snacks while admiring the changing art exhibitions on the walls.

Cocktails and tapas at Museo Chicote

Specialist Restaurants

Dining room at El Buda Feliz 1974

PRICE CATEGORIES
For a three-course meal for one with half a bottle of wine (or equivalent meal), taxes and extra charges.

€ under €35 ■ €€ €35–€70 ■ €€€ over €70

① El Buda Feliz 1974
MAP D3 ■ Calle de Tudescos 5 ■ 915 31 94 24 ■ €

The oldest Chinese restaurant in Madrid has a charming interior and serves beautifully presented traditional and fusion dishes. Wonton soup, lemon chicken and lacquered duck are the highlights here.

② Zara
MAP R2 ■ Calle Barbieri 8 ■ 915 32 20 74 ■ Closed Mon, Sun, public hols, Aug ■ €

Just off the Gran Vía, Zara has been a rallying point for Cuban exiles since the 1960s. It serves Caribbean standards such as *ropa vieja* (stewed meat in a rich tomato sauce) and great daiquiris.

③ Takos al Pastor
MAP N3 ■ Calle de la Abada 2 ■ 636 63 21 77 ■ Closed Mon ■ €

This taco joint is always popular. At just €1 per taco, you can savour flavours of Mexico in every bite. Wash your meal down with a spicy *michelada* (beer mixed with Clamato juice).

④ Aguapanela Restaurante Colombiano
MAP E3 ■ Calle de San Marcos 26 ■ 910 57 35 57 ■ €€

Head here for Colombian flavours in the centre of Madrid, with a vibrant atmosphere and delicious cocktails.

⑤ La Pulpería de Victoria
MAP P4 ■ Calle Victoria 2 ■ 910 80 49 29 ■ €

Specialities at this Galician spot include *pulpo a feira* (octopus) and *empanada* (filled pastry baked in wood-fired oven).

⑥ Restaurante Momo
MAP E3 ■ Calle de la Libertad 8 ■ 915 32 73 48 ■ €€

A Mediterranean restaurant with excellent vegetarian, vegan and gluten-free options, plus wonderful desserts.

⑦ La Venganza de Malinche
MAP P3 ■ Calle Jardines 5 ■ 915 23 41 64 ■ €

Range of spicy tacos, burritos and other Mexican specialities are available here. Complete the experience with a flavoured margarita.

⑧ Yakitoro
MAP E4 ■ Calle Reina 41 ■ 917 37 14 41 ■ €

Run by celebrity chef Alberto Chicote, this popular restaurant often draws long queues. The flavour here is a Japanese-Spanish fusion.

⑨ La Pecera
MAP R3 ■ Calle Alcalá 42 ■ 915 31 33 02 ■ €

For a small entrance fee, you can enjoy flavourful dishes in the Círculo de Bellas Artes café *(see p50)*.

⑩ Lhardy
MAP P4 ■ Carrera de San Jerónimo 8 ■ 915 22 22 07 ■ Closed Sun D & public hols D ■ €€

Founded in 1839 by a Swiss-French chef, the tapas counter downstairs is particularly recommended *(see p68)*.

See map on pp92–3

⓾ Royal Madrid

To wander around this part of Madrid is to be reminded constantly of its regal associations. The magnificent Monasterio de las Descalzas Reales and the Monasterio de la Encarnación are both royal foundations, dating from the Habsburg era (1516–1700), while work on the breathtaking Palacio Real, inspired by the Louvre in Paris, began during the first reign of Felipe V (1700–25). Joseph Bonaparte was King of Spain for only five years (1808–13), but he laid out the plans for the handsome Plaza de Oriente next to the palace. Further afield, the Ermita de San Antonio de la Florida was commissioned by Carlos IV.

Madonna at Monasterio de las Descalzas Reales

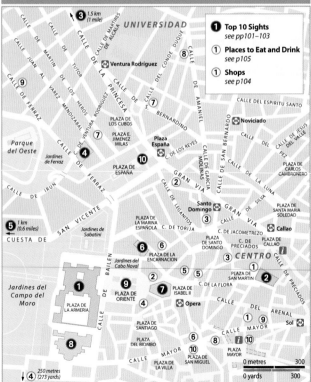

ROYAL MADRID

1 Top 10 Sights
see pp101–103

1 Places to Eat and Drink
see p105

1 Shops
see p104

1 Palacio Real

Spain's magnificent palace *(see pp12–15)* dominates the area.

2 Monasterio de las Descalzas Reales

MAP M3 ■ Plaza de las Descalzas Reales S/N ■ Open 10am–2pm & 4–6:30pm Tue–Sat, 10am–3pm Sun ■ Adm ■ www.patrimonionacional.es

This 16th-century convent is a haven of peace and quiet after the noise and bustle of Puerta del Sol and the Gran Vía nearby. The building started out as a palace, owned by the royal treasurer, Alonso Gutiérrez; in 1555 he sold it to the sister of Felipe II, Juana of Austria, who founded the convent four years later. The nuns were Franciscans, but were known, because of their aristocratic backgrounds, as the "Barefoot Royals". The convent is filled with works of art donated by the nuns' wealthy relatives. The artworks are displayed in the fascinating museum here.

3 Museo de América

Avenida Reyes Catótilcos 6 ■ 915 49 26 41 ■ Open 9:30am–3pm Tue–Sat (to 7pm Thu), 10am–3pm Sun & public hols ■ Closed 1 & 6 Jan, 1 May, 24, 25 & 31 Dec and one local holiday ■ Adm (free Sun and after 2pm on Thu) ■ www.culturaydeporte. gob.es/museodeamerica

Spain's links with the American continent have a long history, and this museum *(see p48)* displays artifacts from all eras, including ceramics, art and textiles.

Museo de América

Exhibits at Museo Cerralbo

4 Museo Cerralbo

MAP J1 ■ Calle de Ventura Rodríguez 17 ■ 915 47 36 46 ■ Open 9:30am–3pm Tue–Sat, 5–8pm Thu, 10am–3pm Sun & public hols ■ Closed Mon, 1 & 6 Jan, 1 May, 9 Nov, 24, 25 & 31 Dec ■ Adm (free Sun, 2–3pm Sat, 5–8pm Thu) ■ www.culturaydeporte. gob.es/mcerralbo

Don Enrique de Aguilera y Gamboa, Marqués de Cerralbo (1845–1922), was a poet, politician and collector, who searched the world for treasures to adorn his palatial home. He bequeathed his collection to the state so that it could be enjoyed by others. Highlights of the museum *(see p48)* include a majolica Nativity by Renaissance artist Andrea della Robbia (in the Sunroom) and El Greco's *Ecstasy of St Francis* (in the Sacristy), but the jewel in the crown is Juderías Caballero's *Allegory of Dance* in the dome of the ballroom.

5 Ermita de San Antonio de la Florida

Glorieta de San Antonio de la Florida 5 ■ 915 42 07 22 ■ Open mid-Jun–mid-Sep: 9:30am–2pm, 3–7pm Tue–Sun; Sep–Jun: 9:30am– 8pm Tue–Sun; closed Mon & public hols ■ www.madrid.es/ermita

Dedicated to St Anthony of Padua, this hermitage was completed in 1798. Goya began work on his frescoes in June, and by December they were finished. On St Anthony's Day (13 June) unmarried girls would come to the hermitage to ask the saint to find them a husband.

6 Monasterio de la Encarnación

MAP K3 ■ Plaza de la Encarnación 1 ■ Open 10am–2pm & 4–6:30pm Tue–Sat (to 3pm Sun) ■ Adm (free 4–6pm Wed & Thu) ■ www.patrimonio nacional.es

The convent was founded in 1611 by Margarita of Austria, wife of Felipe III, for daughters of the nobility. It was also the church of the Alcázar – a picture gallery linked the two buildings. Unfortunately, when the castle was destroyed by fire in 1734, the flames spread to the convent and many of its treasures were lost. A great deal remains however, such as 17th-century paintings by Ribera and Luca Giordano; impressive sculptures, such as *Recumbent Christ* by Gregorio Fernández; embroidered vestments and gold and silverware. The guided tour takes in the cloister decorated with Talavera *azulejos*; the reliquary, where visitors are shown the phial containing the congealed blood of St Pantaleon; the carved stalls in the choir; and the church, designed by Ventura Rodríguez.

7 Teatro Real

MAP K3 ■ Plaza Isabel II ■ Open for tours 10am–3:30pm daily ■ Closed 1 Jan, Aug & 25 Dec ■ Adm (under 5s free) ■ www.teatroreal.es

The city's state-of-the-art opera house has undergone several facelifts over the years. There were so many delays in constructing the original theatre that the architect, Antonio López Aguado, was long dead before the official opening in 1850 on Queen

Teatro Real opera house

Isabella II's birthday. Giuseppe Verdi wrote his opera *The Force of Destiny* for the Teatro Real in 1863 – he stayed at No.6 Plaza de Oriente. The dimensions of the restored opera house are impressive. The backstage area is large enough to contain the Telefónica building on Gran Vía *(see p64)*.

8 Catedral de la Almudena

MAP J4 ■ Calle de Bailén 10 ■ Open Jul–Aug: 10am–9pm; Sep–Jun: 10am–8pm daily ■ Museum & dome: open 10am–2:30pm Mon–Sat ■ Adm ■ www.catedraldelaalmudena.es

Plans to build a cathedral on the superb hilltop site were made in the 18th century, but it was not until 1879 that the Marqués de Cubas was able to execute his ambitious design; even then, only the Romanesque-style crypt was built. The cathedral was finally completed In the 1980s by architect Fernando Chueca Goitia and opened by Pope John Paul II in 1993. The Gothic interior comes as a surprise, as the exterior is Neo-Classical to harmonize with the Palacio Real. The striking double dome offers great views of the city. The magnificent bronze entrance doors were installed in October 2000.

9 Plaza de Oriente
MAP K3

The focal point of this square is the bronze equestrian statue of Felipe IV, moved here from the Buen Retiro palace in 1842. The sculptor Pietro Tacca took advice from Galileo Galilei on the modelling of the rearing horse. The figure of the king was based on sketches by Velázquez. The statues of Spanish rulers were intended for the balustrade of the Palacio Real but they did not meet with royal approval.

10 Plaza de España
MAP K1

A set piece from the Franco era, the huge square at the bottom of the Gran Vía is dominated by Madrid's first skyscrapers, built in the 1950s and extensively reworked in 2021. In the centre, a monument dedicated to Cervantes features bronze statues of Don Quixote and his faithful companion Sancho Panza. Just visible off the northwest corner of the square is the splendid Templo de Debod, erected in the 2nd century BC near Aswan in Egypt and rebuilt here in 1972. The Plaza, renovated and reopened in early 2022, connects eight of Madrid's historic enclaves.

The monument at Plaza de España

A DAY IN ROYAL MADRID

▶ MORNING

Start in **Plaza de Isabel II**, named after the queen who reigned from 1833 to 1868 and whose statue stands in its centre. This is the best place to admire Madrid's opera house, the **Teatro Real**. Follow Calle Felipe V alongside the theatre until you come to **Plaza de Oriente** and the **Palacio Real** *(see p101)*. The palace is closed at least once a week for official functions but, if it is open, it is worth spending an hour here.

There are plenty of places to eat in the vicinity of Plaza de Oriente, for example the **Café de Oriente** *(see p105)*. A plaque on the wall nearby reminds visitors that this was once the treasury house where the artist Velázquez had his studio.

AFTERNOON

After lunch, walk over to the ancient Egyptian **Templo de Debod**, located northwest of Plaza de España. Beautifully reflected in a shallow pool, this stunning temple was a gift to Madrid from the Egyptian government in the 1970s. Continue walking beyond the temple into the quiet, shady paths of the **Parque del Oeste** *(see p52)*, where you'll find the **Teleférico de Madrid** cable car *(see p61)* to the **Casa de Campo** *(see p53)*. From the cable car station, stroll about 30 minutes through the park to reach the lake (follow signs for *lago*), where you can hire a rowing boat or enjoy a drink at one of the cafés.

See map on p100 ←

Shops

Records for sale at La Metralleta

1 La Metralleta
MAP M3 ▪ Plaza San Martín 1-B

This large store specializes in second-hand records. Every taste and period is catered for and the staff are helpful and knowledgeable.

2 Cántaro
MAP L1 ▪ Calle Flor Baja 8

A treasure trove for admirers of pottery and an excellent place to shop for gifts. Products from all over Spain at very reasonable prices.

3 Antigua Casa Talavera
MAP L2 ▪ Calle de Isabel La Católica 2

If you've been bowled over by the 18th-century Talavera ceramics in the Palacio Real, you'll find that the modern descendants of these artisans have not lost their touch. This outlet (see p70) offers a wide range of hand-painted jugs, plates, mugs and more.

4 Guitarras Manuel Contreras
MAP A5 ▪ Calle Segovia 57

This historic workshop (see p70) is where true guitar enthusiasts come to buy a handcrafted instrument.

5 Flamencoexport
MAP C4 ▪ Calle de Campomanes 4

This colourful shop (see pp70–71) specializes in all things flamenco, from beautiful dresses, dance shoes and shawls to guitars and castanets, as well as CDs, DVDs, sheet music and books.

6 La Chinata
MAP L4 ▪ Calle Mayor, 44

An excellent gourmet shop where a wide variety of products ranging from beauty products, oils and candles are available. The prices are reasonable and cater to all budgets.

7 Ocho y Medio
MAP J1 ▪ Calle de Martín de los Heros 11

Located in the centre of Madrid's main cinema district, this bookshop is a treasure house for film buffs, with books, posters, postcards and more.

8 Kukuxumusu
MAP L4 ▪ Calle Mayor 47

This design company started as three friends selling T-shirts on the streets of Pamplona during the 1989 Sanfermines fiesta. The bright graphics proved hugely popular, and Kukuxumusu now sells its products throughout Europe.

9 El Riojano
MAP M4 ▪ Calle Mayor 10

Founded in 1855, this pretty, old-style *pastelería* caters for none other than the Spanish royal family. Shop here for seasonal Madrid specialities such as *tocino de cielo*, a silky-smooth crème caramel.

10 Casa Yustas
MAP M4 ▪ Plaza Mayor 30

Founded back in 1886, this shop has a hat for every occasion, from bowler hats and flat caps to trilbies and beanies. Largely aimed at men, with some items for women and children, the shop also stocks gloves, hatboxes and military accessories.

Places to Eat and Drink

1 Chocolatería San Ginés
MAP M4 ▪ Pasadizo de San
Ginés 5 ▪ 913 65 65 46 ▪ €

Head here after a night out for a
traditional breakfast of *chocolate
con churros*.

2 Taberna del Alabardero
MAP K3 ▪ Calle de Felipe V 6
▪ 915 47 25 77 ▪ €€

Snack on *jamón Ibérico* or *croquetas* in
the tapas bar *(see p66)*, or eat Basque
food in the adjoining restaurant.

**3 Restaurante Sidrería
Casa Parrondo**
MAP D3 ▪ Calle de Trujillos 9 ▪ 915 22
62 34 ▪ €€

A tavern serving seafood caught in
the Bay of Biscay, as well as Asturian
bean stew and classic natural cider.

Plush interior of Café de Oriente

4 Café de Oriente
MAP K3 ▪ Plaza de Oriente 2
▪ 915 41 39 74 ▪ €€

An elegant café with velvet seats, a
stucco ceiling and summer terrace.

5 Entre Suspiro y Suspiro
MAP L3 ▪ Calle de Caños del
Peral 3 ▪ 915 42 06 44 ▪ Closed Sun,
22 & 25 Dec ▪ €€

Delicious and creative Mexican dishes
include *pollo al mole* – chicken breast
prepared in a chocolate sauce with
32 different spices.

6 La Bola Taberna
MAP L2 ▪ Calle de la Bola 5
▪ 915 47 69 30 ▪ Closed Sun D,
24 Dec ▪ No credit cards ▪ €

Cocido (various meats cooked in a
rich broth) is the highlight at this
19th-century restaurant.

PRICE CATEGORIES

For a three-course meal for one with half
a bottle of wine (or equivalent meal),
taxes and extra charges.

€ under €35 €€ €35–€70 €€€ over €70

7 El Jardín Secreto
MAP R3 ▪ Calle Conde
Duque 2 ▪ 915 41 80 23 ▪ Closed
Mon, L daily ▪ €

A hidden gem, El Jardín Secreto has
a terrace café offering light meals
amid an oasis of greenery.

8 El Cangrejero
MAP C2 ▪ Calle de Amaniel 25
▪ 915 48 39 35 ▪ €

This bar has a good choice of
seafood tapas. Mahou beer originally
came from the factory next door.

9 Entrevinos
MAP J1 ▪ Calle de Ferraz 36
▪ 915 48 31 14 ▪ Closed 1 & 6 Jan, 24,
25 & 31 Dec ▪ €

Speciality snacks include *salmorejo*
(cold tomato and almond soup
with spider crab) and omelette with
shrimp and spinach. The wine list
is great.

10 Mercado de San Miguel
MAP L5 ▪ Plaza de San Miguel
▪ 915 42 49 36 ▪ €

An early 20th-century market *(see
p71)* where the best shops have
kiosks selling ham, cheese, sushi,
foie gras and pastries.

Façade of Mercado de San Miguel

See map on p100

ᴛᴼᴾ10 Old Madrid

In the 17th century, the focus of the rapidly growing city shifted from the medieval centre around Plaza de la Paja to Plaza Mayor. Part meeting place, part market, this magnificent square was, above all, a place of spectacle and popular entertainment. Over time the houses deteriorated into slums and tenements, while the parishes to the south of Plaza Mayor were home to Madrid's labouring classes. Mingling with the slaughterhouse workers and tanners of the Rastro were market traders, builders, innkeepers, horse-dealers and members of the criminal underclass.

Plaza de la Paja bronze

OLD MADRID

1	Top 10 Sights *see pp107–109*	1	The Best of the Rest *see p112*
1	Traditional Restaurants and Bars *see p117*	1	Nights Out *see p115*
1	Shops in La Latina *see p114*	1	Places to Eat and Drink *see p116*
		1	Specialist Shops *see p113*

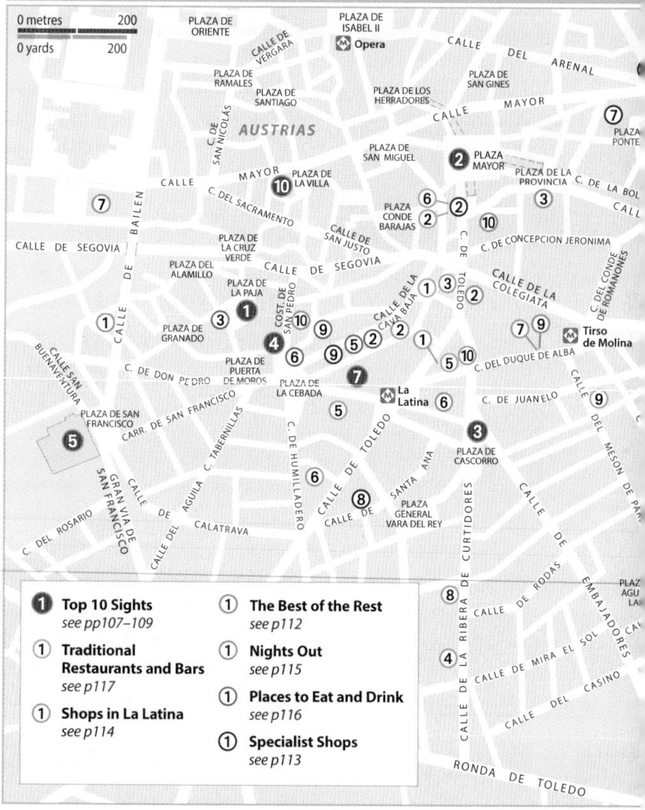

1 Plaza de la Paja
MAP K6

This was the central square and marketplace of medieval Madrid, later eclipsed by the Plaza Mayor. Today, it is one of the prettiest corners of the city, flanked by handsome palaces and cafés that spill into the square in summer. At its northern end is the Capilla del Obispo (the Bishop's Chapel), erected in 1535 as a burial place for San Isidro (whose remains were eventually buried in the Cathedral de San Isidro in the 18th century). The chapel contains a splendid Renaissance altarpiece as well as the elaborate tombs of *Madrileño* aristocrats.

The busy square, Plaza Mayor

2 Plaza Mayor

The heart of Old Madrid is this vast square (see pp22–3), surrounded by arcaded buildings, now home to a good choice of tourist shops, overpriced restaurants and numerous street entertainers.

3 El Rastro

You can easily lose a day wandering around the quirky stalls of the city's flea market (see pp26–7) or watching the world go by from the many bars and cafés of the surrounding La Latina quarter.

4 Museo de los Orígenes (Casa de San Isidro)
MAP K6 ▪ Plaza de San Andrés 2 ▪ Open 10am–8pm Tue–Sun & public hols; mid-Jun–mid-Sep: 10am–7pm Tue–Sun ▪ Closed Mon, 1 & 6 Jan, 1 May, 24, 25 & 31 Dec

The museum is housed in a 16th-century palace, which once belonged to the Count of Paredes. The original Renaissance courtyard is best viewed from the first floor, where archaeological finds from the Madrid region are exhibited, including a Roman mosaic floor from the 4th century. Downstairs, visitors can see wooden models of the city and its royal palaces as they were in the 17th century. A short film is shown bringing to life Francisco Rizi's painting of the 1680 *auto-de-fé* (see p23) and the San Isidro chapel, which was built in the early 17th century near the saint's alleged home.

5 Real Basílica de San Francisco el Grande

Legend has it that this basilica (see pp24–5) occupies the site of a monastery founded by St Francis of Assisi in the 13th century. With a majestic dome and full of works of art, it is one of Madrid's most beautiful churches.

6 Lavapiés
MAP D6

This vibrant neighbourhood, popular with the LGBTQ+ community, has a multicultural feel, owing to its mix of Moroccan, Indian, Turkish, Chinese and Senagalese residents. Its narrow, cobbled alleyways slope up towards the city centre, and the 19th-century *corralas* (tenements) testify to the original working-class population. Today, Arab tearooms, Indian restaurants and Chinese shops abound. Check out hipster and traditional bars such as Taberna Antonio Sánchez (see p66). Lavapiés features some cutting-edge cultural centres. View an exhibition, enjoy a concert or participate in interesting workshops at La Casa Encendida Cultural Centre (Ronda de Valencia 2), one of Madrid's most avant-garde and socially conscious institutions. La Tabacalera de Lavapiés (Calle de Embajadores 53) is another exciting art centre well worth a visit. Housed in a former tobacco factory, it hosts contemporary art exhibitions, sometimes with live music, and is particularly known for the dynamic murals on its walls.

7 La Latina
MAP L6

Historic La Latina really comes alive on Sundays when the trendy bars of Cava Baja, Calle de Don Pedro and Plaza de los Carros are frequented by pop singers, actors and TV stars. Plaza de la Paja – the main square of medieval Madrid – takes its name from the straw which was sold here by villagers from the across the River Manzanares. Nowadays it's much quieter and a good place to rest one's legs. The two churches of San Andrés and San Pedro el Viejo

have been restored. Their history, and that of the area as a whole, is explained in the Museo de los Orígenes (see p107).

Bar in Cava Baja, La Latina

8 Casa-Museo de Lope de Vega

MAP R5 ▪ Calle de Cervantes 11 ▪ 914 29 92 16 ▪ Open for tours in English 10am–6pm Tue–Sun (call or email casamuseolopedevega@madrid.org to book ahead) ▪ Closed Mon & public hols

A key dramatist in 17th-century Spain, Lope de Vega lived in this house from 1610 until his death in 1635. He began writing at the age of 12, producing a total of 1,500 plays plus poetry, novels and devotional works. He became a priest in 1614, but continued his philandering, getting into trouble with the law. To tour the restored house with its wooden shutters, creaking staircases and beamed ceilings is to step back in time. Evocative details include a cloak and sword left by one of his friends in the guest bedroom.

SAN ISIDRO

When the future patron saint of Madrid died around 1170 he was buried in a pauper's grave. But, in the 17th century, an unseemly rivalry developed between the clergy of San Andrés and the Capilla de San Isidro over the custody of his mortal remains. The wrangle dragged on until the 18th century, when the body of the saint was interred in the new Catedral de San Isidro, where it has remained ever since.

⑨ Plaza de Santa Ana
MAP P5

The streets around this well-known square have the greatest concentration of tapas bars in the city and are often still buzzing at 4am. The stylish hotel ME Madrid, home to popular rooftop bar Radio (see p116), dominates the square, and there is an amazing view of the Teatro Español opposite from its penthouse bar. Two statues in Plaza de Santa Ana honour Spanish literary giants – playwright Pedro Calderón de la Barca (1600–81), and poet, playwright and theatre director Federico García Lorca (1898–1936), who was killed by the Nationalists during the Spanish Civil War.

⑩ Casa de la Villa
**MAP K5 ▪ Plaza de la Villa 5
▪ Closed to the public**

Madrid's city hall was inaugurated in 1692, and remained the seat of the city council until 2007. Its austere façade, steepled towers and ornamental portals are typical of the architectural style favoured by the Habsburgs. Juan de Villanueva added the balcony overlooking Calle Mayor so that Queen María Luisa could watch the annual Corpus Christi procession. The Casa de la Villa forms part of an ensemble of historic buildings overlooking the Plaza de la Villa: Casa y Torre de los Lujanes is Madrid's oldest surviving civil building (15th century), and Casa de Cisneros was built for an aristocratic family.

Casa de la Villa

A MORNING WALK AROUND OLD MADRID

▶ Begin the morning at **Plaza de la Villa** with its handsome 16th- and 17th-century palaces. Take the busy **Calle Mayor** as far as Calle de Felipe III, then turn into **Plaza Mayor** (see pp22–3). Cross this magnificent square diagonally, leaving the ancient **Calle de Toledo**, once the main exit route south from the city. On the way look out for the **Casa Hernanz** rope store (see p113) and other charming reminders that this was once an artisans' quarter. Looming on the left is the Baroque **Colegiata de San Isidro** (see p112). Continue to **La Latina Metro**.

Turn and follow **Plaza de la Cebada**, past the modern covered market. Turn right into **Plaza del Humilladero** and cross this square to the adjoining Plaza de San Andrés and its huge domed church. Straight ahead is a 16th-century palace, now the **Museo de los Orígenes** (Casa de San Isidro) (see p107).

Follow the path round the back of the church into Costanilla de San Andrés, a narrow street which opens onto the historic **Plaza de la Paja**, a good area for bars and restaurants. On the corner of Calle de Alfonso VI is the **Colegio de San Ildefonso** whose students chant the results of the Christmas National Lottery in a distinctive sing-song.

By now you'll probably be ready for lunch. Vegetarians and vegans will be tempted by the burgers at **Viva Burger** (Costanilla de San Andrés 16). Other good choices include **La Musa Latina** (Costanilla de San Andrés 12) and **Café Delic** (see p116).

See map on pp106–7

The Best of the Rest

1 Ateneo de Madrid

MAP R5 ▪ Calle del Prado 21
▪ Guided tours: times vary (book ahead) ▪ Adm ▪ www.ateneode madrid.com

One of Madrid's great cultural institutions, the Ateneo was founded in 1835 to promote the arts and sciences. The building contains a library of half a million volumes.

2 Colegiata de San Isidro
MAP M6 ▪ Calle de Toledo 37
▪ Open for services

This imposing church was built in 1622 by the Jesuits. In 1768 the remains of Madrid's patron saint, San Isidro, were interred here.

3 Palacio de Santa Cruz
MAP M5 ▪ Plaza de la Provincia 1

With lovely spires and courtyards, this 17th-century palace was originally used as a prison. It now houses the Ministry of Foreign Affairs.

The striking Palacio de Santa Cruz

4 Teatro Español
MAP Q5 ▪ Calle del Príncipe 25
▪ Closed Mon

Spain's National Theatre began as an open courtyard. Look for medallions depicting the country's best-known dramatists above the entrance.

5 Teatro de la Comedia

MAP Q5 ▪ Calle del Príncipe 14

Despite its name, the Comedy Theatre stages classical plays. The lovely façade dates from 1874, while the auditorium was magnificently restored in the 1990s.

Tapas bar on Calle de las Huertas

6 Calle de las Huertas

MAP Q5

The name of this street refers to the orchards that flourished here in the 17th century. Today it is better known for its nightlife.

7 Muralla Árabe
MAP J5 ▪ Cuesta de la Vega

Remains of the medieval defences are best seen from Parque Emir Mohammad I. The original section dates from the 9th century.

8 La Gatoteca
MAP E6 ▪ Calle Argumosa, 28
▪ Adm ▪ www.lagatoteca.es

Unwind from a hectic day with a non-alcoholic beverage while tickling the ears of a feline friend at this cat café. Book well in advance.

9 Sala Equis
MAP M6 ▪ Calle del Duque de Alba 4 ▪ www.salaequis.es

This cultural space hosts art house film screenings and small concerts. It also has a trendy bar.

10 The Hat Rooftop Bar

MAP M5 ▪ Calle Imperial 9

Set on the roof of a design hostel, this bar offers splendid views. Sip a vermouth and savour the laid-back vibe.

Previous pages The splendid Almudena Cathedral

Specialist Shops

1 La Violeta
MAP Q4 ■ Plaza de Canalejas 6 ■ Open Sep–Jul

This quaint store, founded more than a century ago, sells its own brand of sugared violets, plus a small range of *marrons glacés*, pralines and other sweets.

La Violeta sweets

2 Casa Hernanz
MAP M5 ■ Calle de Toledo 18

An intriguing shop on Calle de Toledo, Casa Hernanz *(see p109)* specializes in items made of rope, including woven baskets and mats, but especially its famous rope-soled espadrilles, available in every colour of the rainbow.

3 La Mallorquina
MAP D4 ■ Plaza de la Puerta del Sol 8

Founded in 1894, La Mallorquina is a famous patisserie. Its specialities are *napolitans* (custard- or chocolate-filled buns), *rosquillas* (ring-shaped sweet buns), truffles and pastries.

4 Casa de Diego
MAP P4 ■ Puerta del Sol 12

The finest in handcrafted fans, exquisite scarves, veils, high-quality walking sticks and umbrellas. This is where Queen Letizia bought the fan for her wedding to King Felipe VI.

5 Franjul
MAP R5 ■ Calle Lope de Vega 11

Choose from nearly 100 different styles and material to custom make shoes of your liking *(see p70)*. You can also design matching handbags.

6 Casa Mira
MAP P4 ■ Carrera de S Jerónimo 30

Founded in 1842 by Luis Mira *(see p71)*, who knew how to cater for the famous Spanish sweet tooth, this *confitería* (confectioner) is best-known for its *turrón*, and also its marzipan, chocolate and *pestiños* (honey-coated pastries).

7 El Ángel
MAP D4 ■ Calle de Esparteros 3

Operating for more than 150 years, this family-run store *(see p70)* is the one-stop shop for religious articles such as rosaries, chalices and painted statues.

8 Guitarreria Manzanero
MAP C6 ■ Calle de Santa Ana 12

Félix Manzanero is one of the finest guitar-makers in Spain, and his charming workshop displays part of his amazing collection of guitars and other musical instruments.

9 Jamones Julián Becerro
MAP L6 ■ Cava Baja 41

This shop offers a variety of Iberian pork products from Salamanca, such as ham and sausages. *Jamón de bellota* (Acorn ham) is considered to be the best. Cheese, foie gras and liqueurs are also sold.

Jamones Julián Becerro

10 Capas Seseña
MAP P5 ■ Calle de la Cruz 23

This iconic store is the world's only shop to sell capes alone. Founded in 1901 by Santos Seseña, today it is run by his great-grandson. The likes of Picasso, Hemingway and Michael Jackson have shopped here. Be warned, these classic Spanish fashion items are not cheap *(see p70)*.

See map on pp106–7

Shops in La Latina

Caramelos Paco
MAP M5 ■ Calle de Toledo 53–55

The display windows of this famous sweet emporium are ablaze with colour and an array of typical flavours such as mojito, gin & tonic and cava to suit all tastes. To be fair to all, sugar-free sweets for diabetics are also created.

Caramelos Paco lolly

El Transformista
MAP C6 ■ Calle de Mira el Río Baja 18

Delve into this treasure trove of antique and second-hand furniture – everything from old mirrors and table lamps to painted plates and plastic chairs.

3 **Calzados LOBO**
MAP C5 ■ Calle Toledo 30

Founded in 1897, this family-run store offers a great selection of Spanish-made shoes, including colourful hand-sewn espadrilles.

4 **Fotocasion**
MAP C6 ■ Ribera de Curtidores 22

Stocks just about everything the photographer might need – cameras (new and second-hand), film, tripods, camera cases and other specialist equipment. Also sells binoculars.

5 **Mercado de la Cebada**
MAP C5 ■ Plaza Cebada 15s/n ■ Open Mon–Fri, Sat am; first Sun of each month

If you want artisanal hams and cheeses but prefer not to go to a tourist spot, try this market (see p71). It is popular with locals, and many of its vendors supply some of Madrid's best restaurants.

6 **Bodegas Mariano Madrueño**
MAP C6 ■ Calle Calatrava 19

For many generations, this small shop has been offering a broad selection of wine and local alcohol, with almost 1,000 products at hand.

7 **El Imparcial**
MAP M6 ■ Calle Duque de Alba 4

Housed in the former offices of El Imparcial newspaper, this shop is part of a cultural centre that also includes a restaurant and bar. It sells gift items, specialist magazines and craft beers.

8 **Nuevas Galerías**
MAP C6 ■ Ribera de Curtidores 12

Shop at this gallery for prints, lithographs, repro-ceramics and antiques. Souvenir hunters looking for unique pieces should make a beeline for Albarelo and Mercedes Cabeza de Vaca.

9 **La EcoTienda Solidaria**
MAP E6 ■ La Casa Encendida, 1st floor, Ronda de Valencia, 2

With a select choice of coffee, tea, chocolate and artwork, this fair-trade shop offers organic products. Its profits go towards projects by the non-profit organization Alianza por la Solidaridad.

10 **La Huerta de Almeria**
MAP M6 ■ Calle de San Millán 2

This small organic shop and café with a smoothie and juice bar sells fresh burgers, wraps, cakes, fruits and vegetables. Vegan products are also available.

Food stalls at Mercado de la Cebada

Nights Out

1 Corral de la Morería
MAP B5 ■ Calle de la Morería 17

Watch flamenco performed by top professionals while dining on superb Spanish dishes at this acclaimed restaurant.

2 Viva Madrid, Taberna Inusual
MAP P6 ■ Calle Manuel Fernández y González 7

Worth seeing for the decorative tiles alone, this tapas bar (see p51) really gets going after 10pm and is popular with the young crowd. Cool off on the terrace in the summer. Note that it becomes busy on weekends.

Flamenco dancer

3 Café Central
MAP P5 ■ Plaza del Ángel 10

Sophisticated jazz lovers enjoy this Art Deco café at the top of Huertas. It hosts live gigs every night from 8pm to 11pm. There is a small admission charge, depending on the artists.

4 La Noche Boca Arriba
MAP E6 ■ Calle Salitre 30

Popular with locals, this nightclub blends vintage decor with barroque. Quirky ambience, a well-priced menu and the DJ-spun tunes here keep the good vibes going.

5 La Negra Tomasa
MAP P4 ■ Corner of Calle de Espoz y Mina, Cádiz 9

The live salsa music, performed from Thursday to Saturday, is the main draw of this Cuban restaurant.

6 El Sótano
MAP C5 ■ Calle de las Maldonadas 6

A trendy and cosy club, El Sótano features an eclectic lineup of both live acts and DJs, with a particular focus on techno and house music.

7 Teatro Circo Price
MAP E6 ■ Ronda de Atocha 35

This theatre (see p51) is named after an Irish horse tamer called Thomas Price who came to Madrid in the 19th century and set up a circus. It is now the best place to see avant-garde performances in Madrid.

8 Commo
MAP P5 ■ Calle de Espoz y Mina 22

This hip, lively club welcomes dancers with its buzzing atmosphere. It plays pachanga, a popular style of music, and offers other varied activities and inexpensive drinks.

Entrance of Tablao Flamenco 1911

9 Tablao Flamenco 1911
MAP P5 ■ Plaza de Santa Ana 15

On a corner of bustling Plaza de Santa Ana (see p109), this exquisitely tiled restaurant (see p51) offers polished and entertaining flamenco performances, combined with a choice of menus and wine, twice every evening.

10 Berlín Cabaret 1930
MAP C5 ■ Calle Costanilla de San Pedro 11

With its cabaret interiors, this venue hosts live shows with drag queens, flamenco dancing and cabaret performances. It's open from Tuesday to Saturday, with music from the 1980s and 1990s.

See map on pp106–7

Places to Eat and Drink

 Venta El Buscón
MAP P4 ▪ Calle Victoria 5
▪ 915 22 54 12 ▪ €

A traditional tapas bar *(see p68)*, decorated with paintings of the poet Quevedo, this place serves Spanish omelettes and fried squid, as well as local tapas *Madrileñas*.

2 La Perejila
MAP L6 ▪ Calle de la Cava Baja 25 ▪ 913 64 28 55

A lovely little bar *(see p67)* serving delicious tapas, wine and coffee.

3 Café Delic
MAP K6 ▪ Constanilla de San Andrés 14 ▪ 913 64 54 50 ▪ Closed Mon ▪ €

With retro furnishings, some of which you can buy at its shop next door, this café serves homemade quiches and salads at lunch. In the evening, it is a popular cocktail spot. Its terrace overlooks a pretty square.

4 Casa Gonzalez
MAP Q5 ▪ Calle León 12
▪ 914 29 56 18 ▪ Closed Sun D ▪ €

Housed in a converted 1930s deli, this popular wine bar *(see p67)* offers a huge selection of wine, *empanadas* (savoury pastries) and ice cream.

5 Casa Lucio
MAP L6 ▪ Calle de la Cava Baja 35 ▪ 913 65 82 17 ▪ Closed 2nd and 3rd week of Aug ▪ €€

It's worth splurging on a meal in this restaurant *(see p68)* renowned for its roasts. Booking ahead is essential.

6 El Bonanno
MAP K6 ▪ Plaza del Humilladero 4 ▪ 913 66 68 86 ▪ €

A Madrid classic, this popular bar is right in the heart of one of the city's liveliest nightlife districts. It draws an alternative, arty crowd, including musicians and actors, thanks to its relaxed vibe and well-priced drinks, including *vermut*.

 La Venencia
MAP Q5 ▪ Calle de Echegaray 7
▪ 914 29 73 13 ▪ €

Sherry is the speciality of this lively bar *(see p65)* serving simple tapas.

8 Alhambra
MAP P4 ▪ Calle de la Victoria 9
▪ 915 21 07 08 ▪ €

Enjoy good Spanish wine and Iberian ham at this atmospheric tapas bar *(see p65)*. It is crowded at weekends.

9 Taberna Almendro 13
MAP L6 ▪ Calle del Almendro 13 ▪ 913 65 42 52 ▪ €

A tastefully decorated tapas restaurant, Taberna Almendro 13 *(see p65)* has an Andalucían theme.

10 Radio Rooftop Bar
MAP P5 ▪ Hotel ME Madrid, Plaza Santa Ana 14 ▪ 917 01 60 00 ▪ €

This stylish rooftop terrace *(see p64)* has two indoor bars, delicious cocktails and extraordinary views.

Fashionable Radio Rooftop Bar

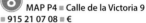

Traditional Restaurants and Bars

PRICE CATEGORIES

For a three-course meal for one with half a bottle of wine (or equivalent meal), taxes and extra charges.

€ under €35 €€ €35–€70 €€€ over €70

1 La Posada de la Villa

MAP L6 ■ Calle de la Cava Baja 9 ■ 913 66 18 60 ■ Closed 1–4pm Sun & Aug ■ €€

This attractive inn dates back to 1642. Traditional Castilian cooking is served. Try the delicious roasts.

2 Sobrino de Botín

MAP M5 ■ Calle de la Cuchilleros 17 ■ 913 66 42 17 ■ €€

American writer Ernest Hemingway was a fan of this restaurant *(see p68)*. His favourite dish, roast suckling pig, is still a house speciality.

3 Cervecería Alemana

MAP P5 ■ Plaza de Sta Ana 6 ■ Closed Tue, Aug

A well-known beer and tapas bar *(see p65)*, Cervecería Alemana opened in 1904 and is still going strong.

4 La Casa del Abuelo

MAP P4 ■ Calle de la Victoria 12 ■ 910 00 01 33 ■ €

This tapas bar *(see p67) par excellence* was founded in 1906 and is still popular. The speciality of the house is prawns.

5 Taberna Oliveros

MAP D6 ■ Calle San Millán 4 ■ 913 54 62 52 ■ Closed Sun D, Mon, Jul, Aug ■ €

Dating back to 1857, this *taberna* *(see p69)* has an old-world charm. It is worth trying the main speciality, *cocido Madrileño* – a stew made from chickpeas, tripe and fried *bacalao*.

6 Taberna de la Daniela

MAP M5 ■ Cuchilleros 9 ■ 913 66 20 18 ■ €

Enjoy traditional cuisine here, such as tapas and *cocido Madrileño* (stew).

7 Casa Alberto

MAP Q5 ■ Calle de las Huertas 18 ■ 914 29 93 56 ■ Closed Sun D, Mon & first week of Jan ■ €

A historic tavern where Cervantes wrote part of *Don Quixote*. It offers *Madrileño* food and vermouth on tap.

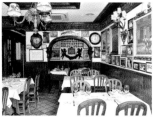

Interior of Casa Alberto

8 Taberna Maceiras

MAP R6 ■ Huertas 66 ■ 914 29 58 18 ■ €

Chaotic and noisy, this restaurant is still well worth a visit for the great seafood, almond cake and wine.

9 Taberna de Antonio Sánchez

MAP N6 ■ Calle de Mesón de Paredes 13 ■ 915 39 78 26 ■ Closed Sun D, 15–31 Aug ■ €

The ambience here is reason enough to visit this traditional inn *(see p66)*. The delicious range of tapas includes black pudding with raisins.

Taberna de Antonio Sánchez

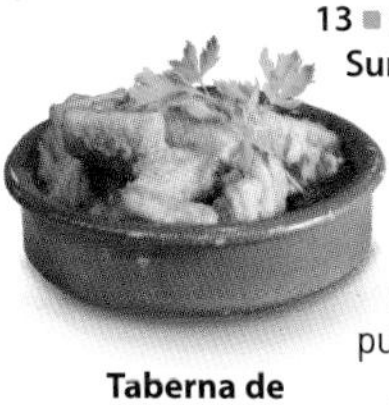

10 Prada a Tope

MAP E4 ■ Calle Principe 11 ■ 914 29 59 21 ■ €€

Traditional classic dishes from the northern Spain region of Bierzo in Leon. Try the meat and the morcilla sausage which is spicy, but worth it.

See map on pp106–7

🔟 Chueca and Malasaña

Two of Madrid's most lively areas lie just off the Gran Vía. Chueca was originally home to the city's blacksmiths and tile-makers. Run-down for many years, it enjoyed a renaissance after being adopted by Madrid's LGBTQ+ community – the area puts on its best clothes in summer for the Pride celebrations. The 19th-century buildings around Plaza de Chueca have been given a new lease of life as trendy bars and restaurants. Neighbouring Malasaña was the focus of resistance against the French in 1808. Like Chueca, it became rather neglected, but is now a trendy neighbourhood and a mainstay of Madrid nightlife.

Art Nouveau detail on Palacio Longoria

CHUECA AND MALASAÑA

1 Casa de las Siete Chimeneas

MAP R2 ■ Calle Infantas 31 ■ Closed to the public

The "house of the seven chimneys" dates from around 1570 and is one of the best-preserved examples of domestic architecture in Madrid. It is said to be haunted by a former lover of Felipe II – not as far-fetched as it sounds, as a female skeleton was uncovered here at the end of the 19th century. The house belonged to Carlos III's chief minister, the Marqués de Esquilache, whose attempts to outlaw the traditional gentleman's cape and broad-brimmed hat, on the grounds that rogues used one to conceal weapons and the other to hide their faces, provoked a riot.

Interior of Museo del Romanticismo

2 Museo del Romanticismo

MAP E2 ■ Calle de S Mateo 13 ■ Open 9:30am–8:30pm Tue–Sat (Nov–Apr: 9:30am–6:30pm), 10am–3pm Sun & public hols ■ Closed Mon, 1 & 6 Jan, 1 May, 9 Nov, 24, 25 & 31 Dec ■ Adm (free Sat after 2pm & Sun)

This museum recreates the Madrid of the Romantic era (c.1820–60), with rooms furnished in the style of the period. Highlights include: fans, figurines, dolls, old photo albums, cigar cases and visiting cards. Among the paintings is a magnificent Goya and a portrait of the Marqués de Vega-Inclán, whose personal possessions form the basis of the collection. The archetypal Spanish Romantic was Mariano José de Larra, a journalist with a caustic pen, who shot himself in 1837 after his lover ran off with another man. The pistol is one of the museum's prized exhibits. There is a lovely garden café on site.

3 Museo de Historia de Madrid

MAP E2 ■ Calle de Fuencarral 78 ■ Open 10am–8pm Tue–Sun (Jun–Sep: until 7pm) ■ Closed Mon & public hols

Once a poorhouse, this museum traces the history of Madrid from ancient times to the present day. Exhibits include mosaic fragments from a Roman villa, pottery from the time of the Muslim occupation, a bust of Felipe II, and Goya's *Allegory of the City of Madrid*. The star attraction is a wooden model of the city constructed in 1830. Note the museum's Baroque portal, dating from the 1720s.

Balcony of Palacio Longoria

4 Palacio Longoria

MAP E2 ■ Calle de Fernando VI,
4 ■ 913 49 95 50 ■ Closed to the public

The finest example of Art Nouveau
architecture in Madrid was created
for Javier González Longoria in 1902.
The architect was José Grases Riera,
a disciple of Antoni Gaudí. Restored
in the 1990s, the walls, windows and
balconies are covered with ornamentation suggesting plants, flowers and
tree roots (see p50). Today this is the
headquarters of the Spanish Society
of Authors and Publishers. The building is occasionally open for guided
tours during Madrid's Architecture
Week in September/October.

5 Iglesia de San Antonio de los Alemanes

MAP N1 ■ Corredera Baja de S Pablo
16 ■ Open 10:30am–2pm ■ Adm

The entire surface area of this
magnificent domed church is
covered with lovely 17th-century
frescoes depicting scenes from
the life of St Anthony of Padua. The
congregation included the sick and
indigent residents of the adjoining
hospice, who were allocated a daily
ration of bread and boiled eggs. The
church still has a soup kitchen, which
feeds around 250 people a day.

6 Teatro Flamenco Madrid

MAP P2 ■ Calle del Pez, 10 ■ 911
59 20 05 ■ www.teatroflamenco
madrid.com

Visitors can immerse themselves
in the enchanting spirit of dance
and music from Andalucia at the
world's first flamenco theatre.
Mesmerizing shows that feature
a range of artists take place
here, along with classes for
flamenco singing, dance, guitar,
castanet and percussion, as well
as the history of flamenco.

7 Plaza del Dos de Mayo

MAP D2

This square situated in the heart
of Malasaña commemorates the
leaders of the insurrection of May
1808, Luis Daoíz and Pedro Velarde,
who are buried at the Plaza de la
Lealtad (see p80). The site was
chosen because, in those days, this
was the artillery barracks of the
Monteleón Palace, the main focus
of resistance to the French. The
brick arch now sheltering a sculpture of the two heroes was the
entrance to the building. Today,
the square is a popular nightspot,
full of fashionable bars and restaurants with terraces.

MANUELA MALASAÑA

The seamstress, who became a
national heroine following the 1808
uprising, was still a teenager on that
fateful day in May, when, so the story
goes, she was approached by a couple
of French soldiers. Despite her protes-
tations, they insisted on conducting
a body search, provoking her to stab
at them with a pair of dressmaking
scissors. They shot her dead, but her
memory lives on in the district which
now bears her name.

Sculpture in Plaza del Dos de Mayo

8 Iglesia San Plácido
MAP N1 ■ Calle S Roque 9
■ **Open for services**

Founded in 1622 by Don Jerónimo de Villanueva, a Madrid nobleman, in its early years this convent was darkened by scandal. Rumours of sexual misconduct among the novices led to an investigation by the Inquisition which implicated the chaplain, the abbess and the Don himself. It was even rumoured that Felipe IV made nocturnal visits here via a tunnel.

9 Palacio de Justicia
MAP F2 ■ Plaza Villa de Paris ■ Closed to the public

Designed by Francisco Carlier and Francisco Moradillo, and constructed between 1750 and 1757, the building served as a convent until 1870. The conversion into the Palace of Justice was carried out by architect Antonio Ruiz de Salces, but its present appearance is due to the restoration work that followed a fire in 1915.

Façade of Iglesia de Santa Bárbara

10 Iglesia de Santa Bárbara
MAP F3 ■ Calle de General Castaños 2 ■ Open 9am–1pm, 5–8pm Mon–Fri; 10am–1pm & 6–9pm Sat, 10am–2pm & 6–9pm Sun & public hols

The monastery of the Royal Salesians was founded by Bárbara de Braganza, the wife of Ferdinand VI, as a refuge from her overbearing mother-in-law should the king die before her (in fact, she died first). The Baroque church (1750) by Francisco Gutiérrez features the tombs of Fernando VI and his wife.

AN AFTERNOON OF CULTURE AND CAFÉS

Begin with a pre-lunch *vermut* at the traditional **Taberna Ángel Sierra** *(Plaza Chueca 11, 915 31 01 26)* and then head into the nearby Mercado de San Antón. Admire the market's fabulous range of produce, then enjoy lunch on its rooftop terrace, 11 Nudos Terraza Nordés.

After lunch, check out the outlet shoe stores along the Calle Augusto Figueroa and the shops on Calle de Fuencarral – you'll find Spanish fashion label, **El Ganso** at No 20 and **Panta Rhei**, a book store with illustrated titles in Spanish and English, at Calle de Hernán Cortés 7. At the top of Calle de Fuencarral, pop into the excellent **Museo de Historia de Madrid** *(see p119)*.

After visiting the museum, stroll along Calle de San Vicente Ferrer, where you'll find some of the city's surviving tiled shopfronts from the 1920s (including a pharmacy at the corner of Calle de San Andrés), and make for the **Plaza del Dos de Mayo**, the historic heart of the Malasaña district. At the corner of the square, **Pepe Botella** *(Calle de San Andrés 12, 915 22 43 09)*, a shabby-chic favourite of artists and actors, is the perfect spot for a *vermut*.

Continue east to the **Centro Cultural Conde Duque** *(see p62)*, a former barracks which has been converted into an excellent cultural centre, and is home to the city's collection of contemporary art. After visiting the gallery, walk to the nearby Plaza de los Comendadoras, where you can join the locals at one of the terrace cafés, such as **Federal** at no. 9 *(915 32 84 24)*.

See map on pp118–19

Fashion Shops

Shoppers browsing the collection at U-Casas

 U-Casas
MAP P2 ■ Calle de Fuencarral 51

This family chain store has a wide selection of shoes for men, women and children.

 Flamingos Vintage Kilo
MAP D2 ■ Calle de San Joaquín 16

A quirky thrift store, Flamingos stocks a variety of vintage clothing for men and women, including denim and suede pants, cowboy boots, leather jackets and Hawaiian shirts. Prices are calculated by the weight in kilos.

 Mott
MAP E3 ■ Barquillo 31

Find original outfits and accessories from a range of worldwide designers at this lovely boutique. Caters for both men and women.

Desigual
MAP P2 ■ Calle de Fuencarral 36

This Spanish brand, started by two Ibizan brothers, has taken the world by storm with their funky, colourful street fashions.

 Foot District
MAP D3 ■ Calle de Valverde 35

Beautifully laid out, Foot District is a popular spot for those who love street wear and trainers. It even houses a special room dedicated to the Air Jordan range available here.

 BAREI
MAP E3 ■ Plaza de Chueca 8

A wonderful store in the heart of Chueca with a wide range of stylish clothes and basic accessories for both men and women. Exclusive brands, great quality and friendly staff.

 La Mona Checa
MAP D2 ■ Calle Velarde 2

This charming shop is packed with a great selection of vintage clothing and accessories. The shop also has an area for art displays, and a collection of old film cameras.

eseOese
MAP E3 ■ Calle de Fuencarral 50

If you prefer neutral colour tones, you will love the clothes, shoes, jewellery and accessories available at this chic boutique.

Delitto e Castigo
MAP F3 ■ Calle de Piamonte 17

Luxury brand store, with unique and exclusive clothes by famous designers such as Roberto Cavalli and Vivienne Westwood.

Proxima Parada
MAP F3 ■ Calle Conde de Xiquena 9

This boutique is the perfect place to shop for occasion wear. Stocking women's colourful dresses, shoes and accessories, many are by Spanish designers.

Specialist Shops

1 Patrimonio Comunal Olivarero

MAP E2 ■ Calle de Mejía Lequerica 1

Spain produces more olive oil than any other country, and this supplier (see p70) stocks the finest Extra Virgin varieties. Also look for the DO (denominación de origen) quality control on the label.

2 Antigua Casa Crespo

MAP D2 ■ Calle Divino Pastor 29

This charming sandal shop was established in 1863. It specializes in traditional espadrilles, hand-woven and sewn by artisans from the La Rioja region of Spain. The shop is often patronized by Spanish royalty.

3 Reserva y Cata

MAP F3 ■ Calle de Conde de Xiquena 13

Interested in Iberian wines? Take care not to overlook this basement merchant with its excellent selection of Spanish wines and liqueurs. Tastings are also on offer.

Reserva y Cata

4 Faraday

MAP E3 ■ Calle de San Lucas 9

Stylish record store with a splendid collection of vinyl records, excellent coffee and a choice of cakes. The owner is a true music lover and offers valuable assistance.

5 Mao & Cathy Tattoo Parlour

MAP D2 ■ Corredera Alta de San Pablo No.6

Mao and Cathy were the pioneers of the art of tattoos in Spain. If you are looking for a long-lasting souvenir, head to this tattoo parlour to get a tattoo by the finest artists in the city.

6 Uno de 50

MAP D3 ■ Calle de Fuencarral 17

With unique handcrafted jewellery designs, for both men and women, Uno de 50 offers something for every budget.

Jewellery on display at Uno de 50

7 Almirante 23

MAP F3 ■ Calle del Almirante 23

Find postcards, perfume containers, tobacco tins, cameras, sunglasses, cinema programmes, menus and cigarette cards here.

8 Tipos Infames

MAP D3 ■ Calle San Joaquin 3

A modern, inviting bookshop with an interesting and eclectic selection of titles. The walls here are hung with changing art exhibitions, and the bookshop even has its own wine bar.

9 Mad is Mad

MAP Q1 ■ Calle Pelayo 48

This Chueca art gallery showcases the work of up-and-coming local artists in a wide range of media, from photography to illustration. The exhibitions are always worth a look, and could provide you with an original and affordable souvenir.

10 Casa Gonzalez & Gonzalez

MAP E3 ■ Calle de Pelayo 86

Bohemian store selling chic goods for the home. A small stationery collection is also available.

See map on pp118–19

Places to Eat and Drink

(1) La Manduca de Azagra
MAP E2 ■ Calle Sagasta 14
■ 915 91 01 12 ■ Closed Sun & public hols, Aug ■ €€€

This restaurant with avant-garde decor is famed for cuisine from Navarre. Enjoy the fresh fish, grilled meats and homemade desserts. Tapas are served at the bar.

(2) YOUnique Restaurant
MAP E3 ■ Calle del Barquillo 21
■ 910 05 22 22 ■ €€

Set in the Only YOU boutique hotel, this restaurant serves a fusion of traditional and modern flavours. Visitors can choose to dine in its elegant interior or outside on the cosy terrace.

(3) Ribeira do Miño
MAP E3 ■ Calle Santa Brígida 1
■ 915 21 98 54 ■ Closed Mon, Aug ■ €€

This back-street Galician restaurant is well-known for its good value shellfish, fresh fish and *Crêpes Suzette*. An assortment of seafood is also available for take away.

(4) El Cisne Azul
MAP R1 ■ Calle Gravina 27
■ 915 21 37 99 ■ Closed Sun D
■ No credit cards ■ €€

Exquisite large tapas are on the menu here. Try the wild mushrooms, rocket salad, lamb chops and steaks.

(5) DSTAgE
MAP E2 ■ Calle Regueros 8 ■ 917 02 15 86 ■ Closed Sat & Sun ■ €€€

Hailed as one of Spain's best dining experiences, go for one of the two taster menus with wine pairings. There's an impressive wine cellar.

(6) Sala Clamores
MAP D1 ■ Calle de Alburquerque 14 ■ 914 45 54 80 ■ €

Enjoy live tango performances, jazz or blues, by renowned artists along with a cocktail at this club *(see p65)*.

(7) Pepe Botella
MAP D2 ■ Calle San Andrés 12 ■ 915 22 43 09 ■ €

Relax and people-watch while having a coffee, beer or glass of wine at this old café with comfortable velvet banquettes and marble-topped tables.

(8) Fábrica Maravillas
MAP P1 ■ Valverde 29 ■ 915 21 87 53 ■ Closed Mon–Fri L ■ €

Equipped with its own brewhouse, this modern space offers many different craft beers on tap. From blonde ale to the most intense, dark Imperial Stout, each type has its own flavour.

(9) Restaurante Vivares
MAP E3 ■ Calle de Hortaleza 52 ■ 915 31 58 13 ■ €

A charming restaurant with a cheerful atmosphere, Restaurante Vivares offers excellent regional cuisine, as well as cocktails. Be sure to try the menu of the day, which is available until late.

(10) Café Manuela
MAP D2 ■ Calle de San Vicente Ferrer 29 ■ 915 31 70 37 ■ €

A club *(see p64)* for young people who drop in to chat, read the paper or play board games. Draught beer, cocktails and snacks are served in the chic 1920s-style interior.

Vibrant interior of Café Manuela

Tabernas

Entrance to Bodega de la Ardosa

PRICE CATEGORIES

For a three-course meal for one with half a bottle of wine (or equivalent meal), taxes and extra charges.

€ under €35 €€ €35–€70 €€€ over €70

1 **Bodega de la Ardosa**
MAP F3 ■ Calle de Colón 13
■ 915 21 49 79 ■ €

A cosy *taberna (see p64)* with Guinness on tap, as well as tapas. Try the *fabes con calamares* (bean and squid stew).

2 **Bodegas el Maño**
MAP C2 ■ Calle de la Palma 64

Head to Bodegas el Maño for delicious food with a great atmosphere and impeccable decor. A must if you are in the Noviciado area.

3 **Casa Camacho**
MAP D2 ■ Calle de San Andrès 4 ■ 915 31 35 98 ■ €

Try the house speciality *yayos* (gin, vermouth and soda water) at this bar operating since 1928.

4 **El Comunista**
MAP E2 ■ Calle de Augusto Figueroa 35 ■ 915 21 70 12 ■ Closed Sun, Mon D ■ €

One of the most traditional *tabernas* in the city, El Comunista offers simple home cooking and a wine shop.

5 **La Trastienda**
MAP R1 ■ Augusto Figueroa 24
■ 913 30 02 71 ■ €

Located within the San Antón market, this bar serves Basque specialities, and at least 15 types of croquettes.

6 **Cervecería La Almudayna**
MAP D2 ■ Calle del Espíritu Santo 5
■ 915 23 51 77 ■ Closed Sun ■ €

Serving a range of great beers, this friendly bar also offers traditional, good-value dishes, including tapas, all made from local ingredients. It is set in the heart of Malsaña.

7 **La Taberna La Carmencita**
MAP E3 ■ Calle de la Libertad 16
■ 915 31 09 11 ■ €€

Known to be the second oldest tavern in Madrid, this place offers more than 75 varieties of classic recipes.

8 **Casa28**
MAP D2 ■ Calle del Espíritu Santo 28

An old butcher's shop converted into a luxurious deli, Casa28 offers a tasting bar of various products, though the meat truly stands out. Excellent wines are also on offer here.

9 **Taberna Ángel Sierra**
MAP R1 ■ Calle San Gregorio 2
■ 915 31 01 26 ■ Closed Wed, 2 weeks in Aug ■ €

Try the *escabeche de atún* (pickled tuna) at this tapas bar *(see p51)*, which has vermouth on tap.

10 **Cervecería Santa Bárbara**
MAP E2 ■ Plaza de Santa Bárbara 8
■ 913 19 04 49 ■ €

Large modern bar *(see p65)*, popular with office workers, serving beer on tap. Good range of tapas.

Cervecería Santa Bárbara

See map on pp118–19

Comunidad de Madrid

The Comunidad de Madrid is a vast region covering 8,000 sq km (3,000 sq miles), with a population now exceeding six-and-a-half million. To the north of the capital is the Sierra de Guadarrama, a majestic mountain range, stretching more than 100 km (60 miles) east–west. Visitors to El Escorial, Valle de los Caídos, or Manzanares el Real will enjoy the superb views as well as the fresh mountain air. An excursion to the university town of Alcalá de Henares can easily be combined with Chinchón. Alternatively you could couple the latter with the fascinating walled city of Toledo, or with Aranjuez, an oasis of gardens and orchards in an otherwise parched landscape.

Aranjuez fountain

COMUNIDAD DE MADRID

❶	**Top 10 Sights** see pp127–9
①	**Historic Places to Eat** see p130
①	**More Places to Eat** see p131

Magnificent El Escorial

① El Escorial

With the famous monastery and views of the Sierra, the attractions of El Escorial (see pp40–43) include the imposing Coliseo, dating from 1771, and the two royal lodges.

② Alcalá de Henares

MAP B1 ▪ Train from Estación del Arte ▪ 91 885 64 87 ▪ University tours: times vary, call ahead ▪ Adm

This town is a UNESCO World Heritage Site due to its wealth of Renaissance and Baroque architecture. It was the birthplace of Miguel de Cervantes, author of *Don Quixote*, and of the ill-fated Queen of England, Catherine of Aragon, the first wife of Henry VIII. The town's importance dates back to the late 15th century when the head of the Spanish church, Cardinal Cisneros, set up a university here. A tour of the buildings, including the main hall with its *mudéjar* ceiling, is a must. Also worth seeing is Teatro Cervantes, the oldest public theatre in Europe, founded in the 17th century and restored in the 1990s.

③ Aranjuez

MAP B1 ▪ Train from Estación del Arte or themed Tren de la Fresa ▪ Palacio Real: open Apr–Sep: 10am–8pm Tue–Sun; Oct–Mar: 10am–6pm Tue–Sun (gardens open 8am–sunset); closed 24, 25 & 31 Dec; adm

This UNESCO World Heritage Site, should not be missed. The Palacio Real, summer residence of Spain's Bourbon rulers, is decorated in the French style. No expense was spared either on the extravagant folly known as the Casa del Labrador, in the grounds near the River Tagus. The town has preserved some *corralas* – balconied wooden dwellings, built around a courtyard. The Mercado de Abastos is good for picnic provisions, and local strawberries, sold at roadside stalls, make the perfect dessert.

④ Manzanares el Real

MAP B1 ▪ Bus no. 724 from Plaza de Castilla ▪ Castle: open 10am–5:30pm Tue–Fri, 10am–6pm Sat & Sun ▪ Garden: open 10am–6pm Tue–Sun (Jun–Sep: until midnight Fri & Sat) ▪ Dramatised visit: 918 53 00 08 (call to book ahead) ▪ Closed 1 Jan, 1 May, 25 & 31 Dec ▪ Adm

A Sierra town, Manzanares el Real is dominated by its well-preserved 15th-century castle. Almost as ancient is the church of Nuestra Señora de las Nieves (Our Lady of the Snow) with its 30-m (100-ft) high belltower. Hikers will enjoy the La Pedriza regional park with its granite boulders.

Majestic Manzanares el Real castle

5 Chinchón
MAP B1 ■ Bus La Veloz no. 337 from Plaza Conde Casal

The centre of this town is the Plaza Mayor, the main square, dating from the 16th century. Originally a cattle market, the square is the focus of a Holy Week (see p74) procession on Good Friday, a passion play on Easter Saturday and bullfights in July and August. Try the local speciality, *anís*, a liquorice-flavoured liqueur (ask for "Chinchón"). It is worth seeing the Iglesia de la Asunción, with a painting of the *Assumption of the Virgin* by Goya, whose brother was the local priest.

Aerial view of Toledo

of St Francis Xavier and the workers' houses, were designed by José de Churriguera himself.

8 El Pardo
MAP B1 ■ Bus 601 from Moncloa ■ Palacio del Pardo: open Apr–Sep: 10am–7pm daily (Oct–Mar: to 6pm) ■ Adm; free for EU citizens & Ibero-Americans (Apr–Sep: 5–8pm Wed & Thu; Oct–Mar: 3–6pm Wed & Thu)

El Pardo is now a suburb of Madrid but was open countryside when Enrico III built a hunting lodge here in the early 15th century. The Palacio Real de El Pardo was built by the Bourbons and enlarged during the reign of Carlos III. More recently, it was the official residence of General Franco, and it is now where visiting heads of state stay. Look out for the tapestries based on Goya's sketches.

Holy week Procession, Chinchón

6 Navacerrada
MAP B1 ■ Bus 691 from Moncloa

At 1,860 m (6,100 ft), Navacerrada is the gateway to the Sierra de Guadarrama. Ski enthusiasts head straight for the Navacerrada Pass (Puerto de Navacerrada), but the town itself should not be overlooked. The parish church has an impressive 15th-century tower. The 16th-century Church of the Nativity and the craft shops are also worth a browse. Cafés abound on Plaza Mayor and there are hiking trails in the forests.

7 Nuevo Baztán
MAP B1 ■ Road: M-219 and R-3

This town south of Alcalá de Henares was the brainchild of an 18th-century nobleman from Navarre, Juan de Goyeneche. He built the estate so that he could supervise his various indus-trial enterprises, which were among the most advanced of the day. The Baroque palace, the domed church

9 Toledo
Road A42 (72km); RENFE train from Estación Atocha ■ www.toledo-turismo.org

Just 30 minutes by express train from Madrid, Toledo is a beautiful walled

---

TREN DE CERVANTES

The Cervantes train is an enjoyable way to see the sights of Alcalá de Henares (see p127). During the pleasant 25-minute journey, hostesses in period costume hand out cakes and snacks, and help visitors. On arrival there is a welcome by musicians, followed by a tour of the old quarter, including the university. Some local restaurants offer discounts to train travellers.

La Pedriza Regional Park 2 km (1 mile)

Restaurante Parra

Calle de Cañada

Plaza del Pueblo

Plaza del Raso

Bus terminal

Castillo Viejo

Manzanares

Calle Real

Our Lady of the Snow

Chapel of the Holy Rock 1.5 km (1 mile)

city crowning a hilltop, and overlooks the Tagus River. It is known as the "city of three cultures", as Christians, Muslims and Jews co-existed peacefully here for centuries. Toledo's most famous resident was El Greco, who never tired of painting the skyline. Some of his works are displayed in the Casa-Museo El Greco but his most famous painting, *The Burial of the Count of Orgaz* (1588), is in the Iglesia de Santo Tomé. The Sinagoga del Tránsito, which holds the Museo Sefardí, was built in the 13th century, and is a jewel of Mudéjar architecture.

10 Valle de los Caídos

MAP B1 ■ Road A-6 north, exit (salida) at M-600 ■ Open Apr–Sep: 10am–7pm daily (Oct–Mar: to 6pm) ■ Basílica: open 10am–7pm ■ Adm; free for EU citizens & Ibero-Americans Apr–Sep: 5–7pm Wed & Thu (Oct–Mar: 3–6pm Wed & Thu)

The "Valley of the Fallen" was General Franco's memorial to those who lost their lives in the Spanish Civil War (1936–9). The crypt and basílica, cut into the mountainside, were built by prison labourers. The monument's most striking feature is a cross, 152-m (500-ft) high and 56-m (180-ft) wide. Franco's remains were buried here after his death in 1975, until 24 October 2019, when he was exhumed in an effort to eliminate public reverance to his dictatorship.

Valle de los Caídos cross

MORNING

To reach **Manzanares**, take bus No. 724 from Plaza de Castilla, alighting at Avenida de Madrid. There's a supermarket near the bus stop if you want to stock up for a picnic. Take Calle del Castillo as far as **Calle de Cañada** and the restored 15th-century castle, from where there are good views of the storks fishing in the reservoir. Return along Calle de Cañada to the old town square, **Plaza del Pueblo**, where you'll find several good cafés and bars if you are ready for a coffee and a rest.

Cross the pretty tree-sheltered Plaza del Raso, passing a small cemetery, and you'll reach the 16th-century Church of **Our Lady of the Snow** with its elegant Renaissance portico. Walk around the church for more views of the lake. Return to **Plaza del Raso** and take **Calle Real**, crossing the River Manzanares to the ruins of the old castle (Castillo Viejo). Then follow the river to the **Chapel of the Holy Rock** *(Ermita de la Peña Sacra)*, built on a huge granite slab. Every Whitsun a procession in honour of the Virgin makes its way here from the cemetery.

Head to the Plaza del Sagrado Corazón and then stroll up to Calle Panaderos for a hearty lunch at **Restaurante Parra** *(see p131)*.

AFTERNOON

Spend a leisurely afternoon enjoying the invigorating, fresh mountain air and splendid vistas of the scenic **La Pedriza Regional Park** *(see p127)*.

See map on p126 ←

Historic Places to Eat

El Charolés
MAP A1 ▪ Calle de Floridablanca 24, San Lorenzo de El Escorial ▪ 918 90 59 75 ▪ €€

At one of the best restaurants in town, with beams dating from the 16th century, chef Manuel Miguez makes his renowned *cocido Madrileño* (a classic, meaty Madrid stew) on Wednesdays.

② Mesón La Cueva
MAP A1 ▪ Calle San Antón 4, San Lorenzo de El Escorial ▪ 918 90 15 16 ▪ €€

Located in an 18th-century house designed by Juan de Villanueva, this restaurant serves fine Castilian cuisine, including delicious roasts.

③ Algóra
MAP A1 ▪ Calle Santa Rosa 2, El Escorial ▪ 696 63 82 24 ▪ Closed Tue ▪ €€

Set in an 1860s train station this restaurant is decorated with exposed brick walls and hardwood floors.

④ Hostería del Estudiante
MAP B1 ▪ Calle Colegios 3, Alcalá de Henares ▪ 918 88 03 30 ▪ Closed Sun D, Mon, Tue ▪ €€

Part of the Parador Hotel, this restaurant is known for its *arroz meloso con sepia y nécora* (creamy arroz with cuttlefish and crab).

⑤ La Cúpula
MAP B1 ▪ Calle Santiago 18, Alcalá de Henares ▪ 918 80 73 91 ▪ Closed Sun D ▪ €€

Set in a Baroque church dating from the 17th century, La Cúpula serves Castilian fare. Several set menus offer excellent value.

⑥ La Balconada
MAP B2 ▪ Plaza Mayor 12, Chinchón ▪ 918 94 13 03 ▪ Closed Wed ▪ €€

Classic Castilian food is served in this 15th century building, which overlooks Chinchón's main square.

⑦ Mesón de la Virreina
MAP B2 ▪ Plaza Mayor 28, Chinchón ▪ 918 94 00 15 ▪ €€

This atmospheric restaurant serves Castilian dishes. Ask for a window or balcony table on an upper floor.

⑧ Mesón Cuevas del Vino
MAP B2 ▪ Calle de Benito Hortelano 13, Chinchón ▪ 918 94 02 06 ▪ Closed Tue, Sun D ▪ €

Housed in an 18th-century olive-oil mill and wine cellar, this restaurant offers a taste of Spain with traditional sierra cooking.

Mesón Cuevas del Vino

⑨ El Rana Verde
MAP B1 ▪ Calle de la Reina 1, Aranjuez ▪ 918 91 13 25 ▪ €€

Charming century-old restaurant perched on the banks of the Tagus River. Traditional cuisine is served with innovative touches. As the name "The Green Frog" implies, frog legs is one of the restaurant's specialities.

⑩ Taberna El Botero
Calle Ciudad 5, Toledo ▪ 925 28 09 67 ▪ Closed Mon & Tue ▪ €€

Housed in a building that is centuries old, the cuisine here has an international influence that lends sensational flavours to old favourites, such as the Thai paella or oxtail lasagna. There are two tasting menus to choose from.

More Places to Eat

PRICE CATEGORIES

For a three-course meal for one with half a bottle of wine (or equivalent meal), taxes and extra charges.

€ under €35 €€ €35–€70 €€€ over €70

 Las Viandas

MAP A1 ▪ Plaza Constitución 2, El Escorial ▪ 918 90 09 86 ▪ €€

Serving seasonal food, this restaurant has a summer terrace where you can enjoy a drink before your meal.

2 **Horizontal**

MAP A1 ▪ Camino Horizontal, San Lorenzo de El Escorial ▪ 918 90 38 11 ▪ Open 11am–midnight Thu–Tue (to 11pm Wed) ▪ €€

This classy restaurant has wonderful vistas of the sierra – book a terrace table in summer. It serves first-class international cuisine.

3 **Restaurante El Reloj**

MAP A1 ▪ Avenida Madrid 20, Navacerrada ▪ 918 42 88 30 ▪ Open 1:30–5:30pm Mon–Fri, 1:30–5:30pm & 8:30pm–midnight Sat & Sun ▪ €

Stylish restaurant serving dishes such as scallop ceviche with mango and baby radishes, or grilled angus steak with roasted pumpkin. Excellent value menu of the day.

4 **Terraza Jardín Felipe**

MAP A1 ▪ Calle Mayo 2, Navacerrada ▪ 918 53 10 41 ▪ Closed Tue, Sun–Thu D in winter ▪ €€

Housed in a stone farmhouse, this restaurant is worth seeking out. Chef Felipe del Olmo is known for his stylish cooking – try the cod with a black garlic alioli sauce. During the summer ask for a table on the large terrace.

5 **Adolfo**

Calle Hombre de Palo 7, Toledo ▪ 925 22 73 21 ▪ Closed Sat & Sun D, Mon ▪ €€

Enjoy updated versions of traditional local recipes in an attractive dining room with beams and deep-red walls.

6 **Rincón del Alba**

MAP A1 ▪ Calle Paloma 2, Manzanares El Real ▪ 918 53 91 11 ▪ Closed Tue–Thu L, Mon–Thu D ▪ €€

Delectable fish and shellfish dishes, plus views of the Santillana marsh and La Pedriza mountain range.

7 **Casa José**

MAP B2 ▪ Calle Abastos 32, Aranjuez ▪ 918 91 14 88 ▪ Closed Mon, Sun D, Aug ▪ €€€

The cuisine at this Michelin-starred restaurant is based on home-grown produce. Try the tasting menu.

8 **Casa Pablo**

MAP B2 ▪ Calle Almíbar 42, Aranjuez ▪ 918 91 14 51 ▪ Closed Tue, 2nd week Jan, 1–15 Aug ▪ €€€

A cosy restaurant, Casa Pablo has the feel of an old tavern. Meat and fresh fish are the specialities.

9 **La Mar Salá**

Calle Honda 9, Toledo ▪ 925 25 47 85 ▪ Closed Sun, Mon–Thu D ▪ €€

Tucked away on the edge of Toledo's historic quarter is this small, romantic restaurant, which specializes in imaginative seafood.

10 **Restaurante Parra**

MAP B1 ▪ Calle Panaderos 15, Manzanares El Real ▪ 918 53 95 77 ▪ Closed Mon, Tue–Wed D, 21 Aug– 12 Sep ▪ €€

Traditional restaurant serving hearty country fare, like *Fabada con almejas* (stew made with beans and clams).

Traditional dining, Restaurante Parra

See map on p126

Streetsmart

Café tables, Plaza Mayor

Getting Around Madrid

Arriving by Air

Madrid's international airport, **Adolfo Suárez Madrid-Barajas**, is 12 km (7 miles) east of the city and is served by all the major national and international airlines.

There are four terminals: T1, T2 and T3 for Air Europa, Ryanair, easyJet and other members of Star Alliance and SkyTeam; and T4 for Iberia and Oneworld Alliance flights. T4 is accessible via free shuttle buses that leave from the other terminals. If your departure gate is in T4S, check in at T4 and take the automatic train to the T4S building.

The Línea Exprés airport bus operates 24 hours a day and departs regularly from outside T1, T2 and T4 to Atocha-Renfe train station in the city centre, with a journey time of around 40 minutes and costing €5. This service operates with reduced hours on 24, 25 and 31 December and on 1 January.

City bus no. 200 runs from 5am to 11:30pm from T1, T2, T3 and T4 to the Avenida de América transport hub, taking about 45 minutes.

Taxis to the city centre take at least 30 minutes and cost €30.

The Barajas metro link (line 8) (open from 6:05am to 1:30am) from T2 and T4 takes 12 minutes to Nuevos Ministerios, and the Cercanía (surburban overground) train runs from T4 to Madrid's main stations, taking about 25 minutes and costing €2.60.

International Train Travel

Spain's international rail services are operated by the state-run **RENFE** (Red Nacional de Ferrocarriles Españoles). Services include TALGO – direct long-distance express trains operated by RENFE – to Madrid from Paris, and a sleeper train from Lisbon. For international train trips, it is advisable to purchase your ticket well in advance. **Eurail** and **Interrail** sell passes to European non-residents and residents respectively for international journeys lasting from five days up to three months. Both passes are valid on RENFE trains.

Domestic Train Travel

RENFE also runs a suburban rail network, Cercanía, to towns around the city – the services are connected at several points with Madrid's metro. They are useful for crossing longer distances within the city, particularly between the two main train stations: Atocha in the south and Chamartín in the north. There are eight colour-coded Cercanía lines, each with a number and the prefix "C". Maps are displayed at stations. Trains run from 5:30am until 11:30pm daily, but hours vary from line to line.

Madrid is also served by four other types of train: regional, largo recorrido (long-distance), TALGO and AVE (a high-speed link to various regions in Spain, which is operated by RENFE).

You can purchase tickets on the RENFE website or at the station. The fastest intercity services are the TALGO and AVE, which link Madrid with Seville in two and a half hours, and with Barcelona in three hours. Iryo and Ouigo now run high-speed services between Madrid and Barcelona. Book at least a month in advance. Trenes regionales y de cercanías (the regional and local services) are frequent.

Long-Distance Bus Travel

Travelling by coach in Spain can quite often be a quicker – and cheaper – way to get around than by train. There are three main long-distance bus stations in Madrid. The Estación Sur de Autobuses, southeast of the city centre, serves the whole of Spain. North of the centre, the Estación Auto-Res operates services to Valencia, eastern Spain, Lisbon and northwest Spain. The Estación de Avenida de América, east of the city centre, serves towns in northern Spain. The transport interchange at Calle de Méndez Álvaro also offers convenient access to buses and trains, linking three local railways, the Estación Sur de Autobuses and line 6 of the metro. Spain has no national coach company, but private regional companies operate routes around the country. The largest of these is **Alsa**, which runs in all regions. Tickets and information for long-distance travel are available at all main coach stations as well as on company websites, but note that it is not always possible to book tickets in advance.

Public Transport

EMT (Empresa Municipal de Transportes de Madrid) is Madrid's main public transport authority. Safety and hygiene measures, timetables, ticket information, transport maps, and more can be obtained at metro stations or from the EMT website. The metro is efficient, and the buses, though slower, are good for short hops.

Tickets

A range of transport tickets is available to choose from to match your particular needs.

The Tarjeta Túristica (Tourist Travel Pass), which can be purchased at the airport, allows you to take unlimited trips on selected public transport for a set number of days. Passes are valid for two zones – Zone A caters for those who plan on travelling within the city, while Zone T is best for those also visiting the surrounding area. The cost varies depending on the number of days and zone you choose.

The Metrobús is a useful multi-ticket – valid for 10 journeys on the bus or metro – it costs €12.20 and can be shared.

Alternatively, you can get a Tarjeta Multi, a contactless, rechargeable card onto which you load passes and tickets. The Tarjeta Multi costs €2.50 and can be shared between people. You'll need to load any single metro tickets and all multiple tickets onto it (unless buying the Tourist Travel Pass). Metro tickets cost €1.50 for five stops and increase thereafter.

Tickets and travel passes are available from most newspaper kiosks, *estancos* (tobacconists) and from ticket machines and staffed booths at metro stations.

Metro

The **Metro de Madrid** is the quickest and easiest way to get around. Thirteen lines serve the whole city and are divided into various zones depending on different areas of Madrid. Work out the direction from the train's final destination; a full list of stops is posted at the entrance to each platform. Operating hours are from 6am to 1:30am daily and trains run every 2 to 5 minutes during peak hours, and every 7 to 15 minutes from 11pm to 1:30am. Note that there is a €3 supplement for travel to and from the airport.

Buses

Madrid has an extensive bus network of over 200 routes. Buses are a good way to see the city but the sheer number of routes can make the bus travel tricky for first-time visitors. Buses can also be slow and crowded, particularly at peak times. Timetables for each line and a plan of the bus network are posted at bus stops. Each bus has the route number on the front. Operating hours are usually 6am to 11:30pm, every 5 to 7 minutes at peak times and every 16 to 24 minutes from 9pm to 11pm, but it depends on the route. Night buses *(búhos)* operate from 11pm to 6am – all routes leave from Plaza de Cibeles.

Buses only stop at designated stops, upon request. When you want to alight, press the button before you reach the next stop. When waiting at a stop, signal to the driver that you wish to board.

Taxis

Official taxis are plentiful, and prices are moderate by European standards. There are taxi ranks at train stations, near the Plaza Mayor, on the Plaza del Sol, along Gran Vía and near the Prado. Taxis can be hailed on the street, or you can pre-book with firms such as **Pidetaxi** or **Tele Taxi** by phone or online.

Taxis are white with a red stripe across the door. A green light on the roof is illuminated when the taxis are available. Look out also for a green sign saying *libre* in the front window. Fares start at €2.50, increasing by €1.10 per kilometre, with supplements for travel at weekends, evenings and for journeys to or from train stations. Be aware that if you call for a taxi, you also have to pay for the journey to the pick-up point.

Trips and Tours

Madrid City Tour buses allow you to hop on or off at major sights multiple times in one day. Services operates from 10am to 6pm between November and February, and from 9am to 10pm from March to October. There are two routes – both cover the Paseo del Prado, after which the blue route heads west around the Palacio Real, and the green route goes north to Salamanca and the Estadio Santiago Bernabéu. Tickets are available for one or two days, and cost €23 for adults, or €10 for those under 16, for one day.

There are also plenty of greener tours to take advantage of in the city. The **Madrid Tourist Office** organizes a wide range of walking tours, including some geared towards travellers with specific requirements. Themes include art and literary tours, haunted Madrid, food and wine tasting, and even crime and mystery tours. Tickets can be purchased at the tourist office, via their website or in some cases at the start of the tour.

Bravo Bike runs city tours with a choice of standard or electric bikes (some streets in the old centre are very steep). It also offers tours of towns outside Madrid, including bike tours of El Escorial, Aranjuez and Toledo.

For a more unusual experience, try a tour by segway. **Segway Tours** runs tours of major sights as well as restaurant- and flamenco-themed excursions. All include an initial training session. Another fun alternative is to scoot around Madrid in a vintage **Seat 600**. There is a choice of three routes, and prices can include lunch or a pit stop for *churros con chocolate* (fried dough strips with hot chocolate). Thrill-seekers can take a helicopter tour with **Heliflight Spain** and marvel at Madrid, Toledo or Aranjuez from the skies.

Driving to Madrid

If you drive to Spain in your own car, you must carry the vehicle's registration document, a valid insurance certificate, a passport or a national identity card and your driving licence at all times. You must also display a sticker on the back of the car showing its country of registration and you risk on-the-spot fines if you do not carry a red warning triangle and a reflective jacket with you at all times.

Many people drive to Spain via the French motorways. From the UK there are also car ferries from Plymouth to Santander and from Portsmouth to Bilbao.

Spain in general has two types of motorway: *autopistas*, which are toll roads, and *autovías*, which are toll-free. You can establish whether a motorway is toll-free by the letters that prefix the number of the road: A = free motorway, AP = toll motorway.

Carreteras nacionales, Spain's main roads, have black-and-white signs and are designated by the letter N (Nacional) plus a number. Those with Roman numerals start at the Puerta del Sol in Madrid, and those with ordinary numbers have kilometre markers giving the distance from the provincial capital.

Carreteras comarcales, secondary roads, have a number preceded by the letter C. Other minor roads have numbers preceded by letters representing the name of the province, such as the LE1313 in Lleida.

From whichever direction you approach Madrid, make sure you are able to identify your motorway turn-off by its street name. Madrid has two major ring roads, the outer M40 and the inner M30. If you need to cross the city, it is advisable to take one of the two and get as close as possible to your destination before turning off. Highways lead to the M30 but most do not continue into the city.

Driving in Madrid

There are restrictions to driving and parking in central Madrid owing to the Madrid 360 low-emission initiative, which allows only electric and hybrid vehicles to drive and park in the central zone. Whole swathes of the city centre have been pedestrianized or are open only to drivers who are residents and whose vehicles meet these criteria. Your hotel may be part of the Madrid 360 scheme that offers one-day passes to visitors, but it's best to check ahead. Otherwise, you're better off paying for an under-ground car park on the outskirts or avoiding driving altogether.

Car Rental

The most popular car-hire companies in Spain are **Europcar**, **Avis** and **Hertz**. All have offices at airports and major train stations. Fly-drive, an option for two or more travellers where car hire is included in the cost of your airfare, can be arranged by travel agents and tour operators.

A car for hire is called a *coche de alquilererer*. You will need an inter-national driver's licence (if you are an EU citizen your ordinary licence is sufficient) and you must be over 21 years of age.

You are also strongly advised to take out full insurance.

Rules of the Road

Most traffic regulations and warnings in Spain are represented on signs by easily recognized symbols. However, a few road rules and signs may be unfamiliar to some non-Spanish drivers. Watch out for blue and white curbs meaning you are not allowed to park.

In Spain you drive on the right side of the road. If you have accidentally taken the wrong road and it has a solid white line, you can turn round as indicated by a *cambio de sentido* sign. At crossings, give way to all oncoming traffic unless a sign indicates otherwise.

The blood-alcohol concentration (BAC) limit is 0.5 mg/ml and is very strictly enforced.

Cycling

Madrid is gradually becoming more bike-friendly, with an increas-ing number of cycle lanes. Cycling around parks like the Retiro or Casa de Campo tends to be a lot safer than on the roads. Experienced cyclists could try the Anillo Verde Ciclista (Green Cycling Ring), a 60-km- (37-mile-) long bike path surrounded by trees that rings the city.

BiciMad is a public bicycle sharing scheme with over 120 stations in the city. Fares start at €2 per hour. Centrally located private firms that offer bike tours and rentals include **Trixi** and **Bike Spain**.

Walking

Madrid is easy to explore on foot and this is one of the best ways to get around and soak up the city's charm and atmosphere. The historic centre is compact and most of the main attra-ctions are within a 20- minute walk of the Puerta del Sol. Many of the central streets have been pedestrianized to combat traffic pollution.

DIRECTORY

TAXIS
Pide Taxi
📞 915 478 200
🌐 pidetaxi.es

Tele Taxi
📞 913 712 131
🌐 tele-taxi.es

TRIPS AND TOURS
Bravo Bike
🌐 bravobike.com

Heliflight Spain
🌐 heliflightspain.com

Madrid City Tour
🌐 madridcitytour.es

Madrid Tourist Office
🌐 esmadrid.com

Seat 600
🌐 600tourmadrid.com

Segway Tours
🌐 madrid-segway.com

CAR RENTAL
Avis
🌐 avis.com

Europcar
🌐 europcar.com

Hertz
🌐 hertz-europe.com

CYCLING
BiciMad
🌐 bikimad.com

Bike Spain
🌐 bikespain.com

Trixi
🌐 trixi.com

Practical Information

Passports and Visas

For entry requirements, including visas, consult your nearest Spanish embassy or check the **Spanish Ministry of Foreign Affairs** website.

From late 2023, citizens of the UK, US, Canada, Australia and New Zealand do not need a visa for stays of up to three months, but must apply in advance for the European Travel Information and Authorization System (**ETIAS**). EU nationals do not need a visa or an ETIAS.

Government Advice

Now more than ever, it is important to consult both your and the Spanish government's advice before travelling. The **UK Foreign, Commonwealth & Development Office (FCDO)**, the **US Department of State**, the **Australian Department of Foreign Affairs and Trade** and the **Spanish Ministry of Health** offer the latest information on security, health and local regulations.

Customs Information

You can find information on the laws relating to goods and currency taken in or out of Spain on **España** (Spain's official tourism) website. For EU citizens there are no limits on goods that can be taken into or out of Spain, provided that they are for personal use.

Insurance

We recommend that you take out a comprehensive insurance policy covering theft, loss of belongings, medical care, cancellations and delays, and read the small print carefully. EU citizens are eligible for free emergency medical care in Spain provided they have a valid European Health Insurance Card (EHIC) or UK Global Health Insurance Card (GHIC).Note that dental care in Spain is not covered by EU health agreements.

Health

Spain has a world-class healthcare system. Emergency medical care in Spain is free for all EU and UK citizens with an EHIC or GHIC. Be sure to present this as soon as possible. You may have to pay for treatment and reclaim the money later. For other visitors, payment of medical expenses is the patient's responsibility. It is therefore important to arrange comprehensive medical insurance before travelling. Ideally, bring a card in Spanish if you have a serious health issue.

No vaccinations are required for visiting Spain. Unless otherwise stated, tap water is safe to drink.

Madrid's main hospitals with *Urgencias* (casualty departments) are **Hospital General Gregorio Marañón** and **Hospital La Paz**. Other hospitals are listed on the **Angloinfo** website, where you can also find dentists and doctors. For an English-speaking doctor or dentist contact the **Unidad Médica Angloamericana**.

An illuminated green cross indicates a pharmacy and these are usually open from 10am to 2pm, and 5pm to 8pm Monday to Saturday, while some are open all day. If closed, the address of the nearest alternative will be displayed in the window. Pharmacists will treat minor ailments as well as give medical advice – most speak a little English – but bring any prescription medicines with you as you may not be able to find the exact equivalent. Pharmacists can also provide information about nearby health centres and doctors.

Ask at your hotel or consult Angloinfo for the nearest dentist. **UDM Clínica Dental** covers 24-hour emergencies. Expect to pay at the time of treatment.

Smoking, Alchohol and Drugs

Smoking is banned in enclosed public spaces and is a fineable offence. You can still smoke on the terraces of bars and restaurants. Spain has a relaxed attitude towards alcohol consumption, but it is frowned upon to be openly drunk. In Madrid it is common to drink on the street outside the bar of purchase.

Recreational drugs are illegal, and possession of even a very small quantity can lead to an extremely hefty fine. Amounts that suggest an intent to supply drugs to other people can lead to custodial sentences.

ID

By law you must carry identification with you at all times in Spain. A photocopy of your passport should suffice. If stopped by the police you may be asked to report to a police station with the original document.

Personal Security

Madrid is generally a safe city, with little crime. Avoid travelling alone at night on empty streets or in metro carriages. As in most cities, pickpockets target people in crowds and at tourist sights; keep your wallet out of sight and don't hang bags on the back of your chair in restaurants. Be careful of scams, such as strangers who tell you that you've dropped something.

To report a theft, go to the nearest police station (comisaría); police stations are listed in the Yellow Pages. Get a copy of the crime report in order to make an insurance claim. The **Foreign Tourist Assistance Service (SATE)** in the National Police Station offers multilingual assistance, including help with filling out crime reports, from 9am to midnight, daily. If you lose your passport, contact your embassy or consulate.

For emergency **police**, **fire** or **ambulance**, call 112. The direct number for the **National Police** is 091, and for the **Municipal Police** it is 092.

Madrileños are generally not the most careful of drivers. Keep an eye open for cars turning from side roads when crossing at street corners.

Madrid is one of the most diverse and progressive cities in Europe. Homosexuality has been legal in Spain since 1979 and Spain was the third country in the world to legalize same-sex marriage, in 2005. In 2006, the Spanish government also recognized the right to legally change your gender. Madrid has a large LGBT+ population and a flourishing scene, centred on the Chueca and Lavapiés neighbourhoods. The city's Pride week, **Madrid Pride**, is the biggest of its kind in Europe, but there are also many other events throughout the year, including **Gayday Madrid**, usually held in September, and **LesGaiCineMad**, an LGBT+ film festival.

DIRECTORY

PASSPORTS AND VISAS

Spanish Ministry of Foreign Affairs
w exteriores.gob.es

ETIAS
w etiasvisa.com

GOVERNMENT ADVICE

Australian Department of Foreign Affairs and Trade
w smartraveller.gov.au

Spanish Ministry of Health
w mscbs.gob.es

UK Foreign, Commonwealth & Development Office (FCDO
w gov.uk/foreign-travel-advice

US Department of State
w travel.state.gov

CUSTOMS INFORMATION

España
w spain.info

INSURANCE

GHIC
w ghic.org.uk

HEALTH

Angloinfo
w angoinfo.com/madrid

Hospital General Gregorio Marañón
Calle Dr Esquerdo 46
(915 86 80 00

Hospital La Paz
Paseo de la Castellana 261
(917 27 70 00

UDM Clínica Dental
Calle Bretón de los Herreros 32
w udm.edu.mx

Unidad Médica Angloamericana
Calle Conde de Aranda 1
w unidadmedica.com

PERSONAL SECURITY

Foreign Tourist Assistance Service (SATE)
National Police Station,
Calle de Leganitos 19
(902 102 112

GayDay Madrid
w gaydaymadrid.es

LesGaiCineMad
w lesgaicinemad.com

Madrid Pride
w madridorgullo.com

Municipal Police
(092

National Police
(091

Police, Fire, Ambulance
(112

Travellers with Specific Requirements

Madrid's facilities are constantly improving. COCEMFE (Confederación Española de Personas con Discapacidad Física y Orgánica) provides useful information for those with reduced mobility, sight or hearing. The Madrid Tourist Office's website has an **Accessible Spain** section with a down-loadable PDF listing the city's attractions and transport options and their accessibility, as well as accessible restaurants.

Madrid's public transport system generally caters for all passengers, with wheelchairs, adapted toilets and reserved car parking available at airports and stations. Trains and most buses accommodate wheelchair users, and metro maps in Braille are available from **ONCE** (Organización Nacional de Ciegos).

Time Zone

Madrid is on Central European Time, an hour ahead of GMT, and six hours ahead of Eastern Standard Time. Spanish summer time begins on the last Sunday in March and ends on the last Sunday in October.

Money

The official currency of Spain is the euro (€). Most establishments accept major credit, debit and prepaid currency cards. Contactless payments are common in the city, but it's always a good idea to carry cash for smaller items like coffee, or when visiting Madrid's many markets. ATMs are widely available throughout the city, although many do apply a charge for cash withdrawals.

Spain does not have a big tipping culture, but tipping is appreciated. Typically, a tip of 5–10 per cent of the total bill in restaurants and €1 per bag or day for hotel porters and housekeeping is usual. It is sufficient to round up to the nearest euro for taxis.

Electrical Appliances

The local power supply is 220 volts AC. Wall sockets have two-pin plugs. Use an adaptor for all electric appliances, such as hair-dryers, shavers and lap-tops. If you are using an American appliance you'll need a transformer.

Mobile Phones and Wi-Fi

Free Wi-Fi is reasonably common in Madrid, particularly in large public spaces, libraries, restaurants and bars. Many hotels provide free Wi-Fi to guests. **WiFi Map** is a handy app that finds free Wi-Fi hotspots that are near you.

Visitors with EU tariffs are able to use their devices in Madrid without being affected by roaming charges. Users will be charged the same rates for data, calls and texts as at home. Those not on EU tariffs should check roaming rates with their provider. A cheaper option may be to purchase a Spanish SIM card.

Postal Services

Correos is the main postal system in Spain. The main post office in Madrid is located at Paseo del Prado 1, and is open from 8:30am until 9:30pm Monday to Friday, and from 8:30am to 2pm on Saturdays. There are several other branches around the city, which are usually open from 9:30am to 8:30pm Monday to Friday, and from 9:30am to 1pm on Saturdays. Postboxes (buzones) are yellow, and are emblazoned with the "Correos" logo in dark blue. Letters sent from a post office usually arrive more quickly than if posted in a postbox. Urgent or important post can be sent by urgente (express) or certificado (registered) mail.

Weather

Madrid sits on a high plateau and has cold winters and very hot, dry summers. The most temperate weather is in spring and autumn. January and February are the coldest months, with average temperatures ranging between 0° and 10° Celsius (32°–50° Fahrenheit). July and August can reach 40° Celsius (95° Fahrenheit).

Opening Hours

Most Madrileños take their annual summer holidays in august. While most tourist sights remain open, many bars and restaurants are closed.

In general, the shops in Madrid are open Monday to Saturday from 10am to 2pm, and 5pm to 8:30pm.

Most central shops are also open on Sundays and holidays. Opening hours for department stores and larger shops and chains are Monday to Sunday 10am to 9pm. Museums have their own opening hours, although many are closed on Mondays.

Public holidays in Madrid are: New Year's Day (1 Jan), Epiphany (6 Jan), Feast of San José (19 Mar), Maundy Thursday, Good Friday, Labour Day (1 May), Feast of the Community of Madrid (2 May), Feast of San Isidro (15 May), Ascension Day (15 Aug), Hispanic Day (12 Oct), All Saints' Day (1 Nov), Our Lady of Almudena Day (9 Nov), Constitution Day (6 Dec), Immaculate Conception (8 Dec), and Christmas Day (25 Dec).

The COVID-19 pandemic proved that situations can change suddenly. Always check before visiting attractions and hospitality venues for up-to-date hours and booking requirements.

Visitor Information

The main **Madrid Tourist Office**, located in Plaza Mayor, is well-stocked with maps and brochures. There are smaller tourist offices at Atocha and Chamartín railway stations, Plaza de Cibeles, Plaza del Callao and Plaza de Colón. Adolfo Suárez Madrid-Barajas airport (see p134) has two information centres in Terminals 1 and 4. Yellow information stands are also located in other terminals. The **Comunidad de Madrid** also has tourist offices, and can provide information on the Greater Madrid area.

The Madrid Tourist Office website has a number of free publications that can be downloaded, including maps, guides, ideas for walks and information on day trips, as well as the free monthly magazine which provides information about what's on in the city.

Local Customs

In Spain women greet other women and men with a kiss on each cheek to say hello and goodbye, while men shake hands with each other.

A famous Spanish tradition is the siesta, which sees many shops close between 1pm or 2pm and 5pm.

Language

Castellano (Castilian) is Spain's primary language, and is the language you will hear most frequently in Madrid.

Taxes and Refunds

IVA (VAT) is normally 21 per cent, but with lower rates for certain goods and services. Under certain conditions, non-EU citizens can claim a rebate of these taxes. Retailers will give you a form to fill out, which you can then present to a customs officer with your receipts as you leave. Some shops offer DIVA (digital stamping technology), which can be validated at self-service machines in the airport.

Accommodation

Madrid offers a huge range of accommodation to suit any budget. A list of accommodation can be found on the **España** website. Book well in advance if you plan to visit in the peak season (July and August). Rates are also higher during major fiestas in the city. Also bear in mind that most hotels quote their prices without including tax (IVA), which is 10 per cent.

DIRECTORY

TRAVELLERS WITH SPECIFIC REQUIREMENTS

Accessible Spain
w accessiblespain
travel.com

COCEMFE
w cocemfe.es

ONCE
w once.es

MOBILE PHONES AND WI-FI

WiFi Map
w wifimap.io

POSTAL SERVICES

Correos
w correos.es

VISITOR INFORMATION

Comunidad de Madrid
w turismomadrid.es

Madrid Tourist Office
w esmadrid.com

ACCOMMODATION

España
w spain.info

Places to Stay

PRICE CATEGORIES

For a standard, double room per night (with breakfast if included), taxes and extra charges.
....
€ under €120 ■ €€ 120–240 ■ €€€ over €240

Luxury Hotels

Barceló Emperatriz

Calle de López de Hoyos 4 ■ 913 42 24 90 ■ www.barcelo.com ■ €€
Guests can expect the very best amenities and stellar service at this cosmopolitan hotel, which opened in 2016. Rooms include 48" TVs and super king beds, and there's even portable Wi-Fi that can be used throughout the city. A drink by the rooftop pool, with its spectacular views, is a must.

Gran Hotel Inglés

MAP E4 ■ Calle Echegaray, 8 ■ 913 60 00 01 ■ www.granhotelingles.com ■ €€€
A unique boutique hotel located in the centre of Madrid, the Gran Hotel Inglés combines modern, urban vibes with Art-Deco touches. Savour the best cocktails at the city's cocktail bar, LobByto, housed in this hotel. Facilities include a spa, a fitness centre and a jet pool.

Gran Meliá Fénix

MAP G2 ■ Calle Hermosilla 2 ■ 912 76 47 47 ■ www.melia.com ■ €€€
This gorgeous hotel near Plaza Colón houses one of the best bars in the world - the Dry Martini Bar. It is handy for the sights and the Salamanca shopping district.

Hotel Hospes Puerta Alcalá

MAP G3 ■ Pl de la Independencia 3 ■ 914 32 29 11 ■ www.hospes.com ■ €€€
Overlooking the Retiro Gardens, this boutique hotel is ideally located for shopping in Salamanca or for visiting the Prado. A sumptuous mansion-turned-hotel, its chic guest rooms are complemented by a spa, a plunge pool and an elegant restaurant.

Mandarin Oriental Ritz

MAP F4 ■ Plaza de la Lealtad 5 ■ 917 01 67 67 ■ www.mandarinoriental.com ■ €€€
Madrid's oldest luxury hotel (see p80) offers refined comfort and impeccable service. The *belle époque* decor and furnishings are seen to best effect in the restaurant, which overlooks a garden. Facilities include a gym and a sauna.

The Principal

MAP R3 ■ Calle Marqués de Valdeiglesias 1 ■ 915 21 87 43 ■ www.theprincipalmadridhotel.com ■ €€€
This occupies a splendid century-old building, and features elegant, contemporary rooms, a fabulous rooftop terrace and a restaurant with Michelin-starred chef Ramón Freixa at the helm.

Rosewood Villa Magna

MAP G2 ■ Paseo de la Castellana 22 ■ 915 87 12 34 ■ www.rosewoodhotels.com/en/villa-magna ■ €€€
What attracts celebrities to this hotel is the service and attention to detail. The restaurant offers a fine dining experience, and the 150 rooms are spacious and elegant. Facilities include a spa and a 24-hour gym.

Villa Real

MAP E4 ■ Plaza de las Cortes 10 ■ 914 20 37 67 ■ www.hotelvillareal.com ■ €€€
This hotel in the heart of Madrid has elegant decor that fuses the classic with the modern. The foyer is decorated with Roman mosaics. Facilities include a fitness suite, conference centre and a gourmet restaurant.

Wellington Hotel & Spa

MAP G3 ■ Calle Velázquez 8 ■ 915 75 44 00 ■ www.hotel-wellington.com ■ €€€
During the San Isidro (see p74) festival in May, this hotel is the first choice for many. Its Michelin-starred restaurant, Kabuki, serves Japanese–Spanish fusion cuisine. It has its own vegetable garden with alfresco dining. The swimming pool is a bonus.

The Westin Palace

MAP E4 ■ Plaza de las Cortes 7 ■ 913 60 80 00 ■ www.westinpalacemadrid.com ■ €€€
This hotel opened in 1913 and has been wowing guests ever since with its

opulence. Soak up the palatial surroundings and enjoy a wide range of cocktails at the Palace Bar. Guests can also avail the spa facilities.

Historic Hotels

Casa Rural & Spa La Graja

MAP B1 ▪ Calle del Paje, 7 ▪ 687 31 78 66 ▪ www. lagraja.com ▪ €

Just a short distance away from Madrid, Casa Rural & Spa La Graja is set in a 19th-century farmhouse, in Chinchón. This lovely guesthouse offers rooms with a rustic charm and historic elements. Various facilities including a spa, free Wi-Fi and a swimming pool are also available.

Eurostars Palacio Buenavista

MAP A2 ▪ Calle de los Concilios 1, Toledo ▪ 925 28 98 00 ▪ www. eurostarshotels.com ▪ €€

Set in a 16th-century palace overlooking the Tagus, this sumptuous hotel has all the modern comforts with period features, such as a stunning stained glass ceiling in the lobby. There's a pool, spa, wellness centre and free Wi-Fi throughout.

Iberostar Las Letras Gran Vía

MAP Q3 ▪ Gran Vía 11 ▪ 915 23 79 80 ▪ www. hoteldelasletras.com ▪ €€

This hotel occupies a Neo-Classical building which preserves its original sweeping staircase and elaborate mouldings. The hotel also has a well-stocked library. The walls of the modern rooms are inscribed with quotes by famous writers, and many

rooms have a private terrace and jacuzzi. Don't miss the views from the chic rooftop terrace.

NH Palacio de Tepa

MAP P5 ▪ Calle de San Sebastián 2 ▪ 913 89 64 90 ▪ www.nh-hotels.com ▪ €€

In Madrid's famous Barrio de las Letras, this 19th-century townhouse has been transformed into a contemporary boutique hotel with a modern interior. Beamed ceilings, elaborate columns and floor-to-ceiling windows in some rooms recall its glory days.

Petit Palace Posada del Peine

MAP M4 ▪ Calle de Postas 17 ▪ 915 23 81 51 ▪ www. petitpalaceposadadel peine.com ▪ €€

This hotel, founded in 1610, is the oldest in Spain and is located on a pedestrian street in the heart of Old Madrid. Some rooms are small, but the decor is modern and iPads are available on request, plus Mi-Fi (portable Wi-Fi) for use throughout the city. Small pets are allowed.

AC Palacio del Retiro

MAP G4 ▪ Calle de Alfonso XII 14 ▪ 915 23 74 60 ▪ www.marriott. com ▪ €€€

In a handsome mansion dating back to 1907, this hotel offers views of the Retiro Gardens. Charming rooms pair period details, such as ceiling mouldings and hardwood floors, with 21st-century extras including iPod docks and plasma TVs. A restaurant and spa are among the other amenities.

Catalonia Plaza Mayor

MAP N5 ▪ Calle de Atocha 36 ▪ 913 69 44 09 ▪ www.cataloniahotels. com ▪ €€

The Catalonia Plaza Mayor could not be more central. This great hotel is set in a 19th-century building just a few steps from the famous Plaza Mayor. The interiors are resolutely modern, but the twirling wrought-iron balconies have been preserved. Extra benefits include a tranquil court-yard and fitness centre.

Gran Melia Palacio de los Duques

MAP L3 ▪ Cuesta Santo Domingo 5 ▪ 912 76 47 47 ▪ www.melia.com ▪ €€€

Originally a 19th century palace, this gorgeous hotel and its expansive garden now provide a plush stay in the heart of Madrid. The hotel has a top-floor pool, three excellent restaurants and a wellness centre. Large beds offer extra comfort in the bedrooms.

NH Collection Madrid Suecia

MAP R3 ▪ Calle Marqués de Casa Riera 4 ▪ 912 00 05 70 ▪ www.nh-collection.com ▪ €€€

The original Hotel Suecia was opened in the 1950s by the Swedish royal family, and famous former guests have included Ernest Hemingway and Che Guevara. After years of neglect, it was bought and remodelled into a stylish, contemporary hotel in 2014, and now offers chic guest rooms and a rooftop terrace with a plunge pool.

Relais & Châteaux Orfila

MAP F2 ■ Orfila 6 ■ 917 02 77 70 ■ www.hotel orfila.com ■ €€€

Built in 1886 as a palatial townhouse, the Orfila is located in a leafy part of town near Colón. The 20 rooms and 12 suites are tastefully decorated in soft pinks and yellows to create a relaxed ambience. A small restaurant over-looks a secluded garden.

Design Hotels

Abalú

MAP M1 ■ Calle del Pez 19 ■ 915 31 47 44 ■ www. hotelabalu.com ■ €€

Each room and apartment has been individually designed in a colourful, eclectic style. Some rooms also have a private balcony. The stylish suites have a separate lounge with a home cinema, and bathrooms with a jacuzzi or Thai stone bath.

Hostal Gala

MAP L3 ■ Costanilla de los Ángeles 15, 2a ■ 915 41 96 92 ■ www. hostalgala.com ■ €€

If you're looking for style on a budget, this guest-house is a great choice. The air-conditioned rooms and apartments are compact, but feature chic, modern decor, and the friendly staff go out of their way to make guests feel at home.

Hotel Santo Domingo

MAP L2 ■ Calle de San Bernardo 1 ■ 915 47 98 00 ■ www.hotelssanto domingo.es ■ €€

This hotel, convenient for the Palacio Real and the Gran Vía, has thematic and colour

therapy-inspired rooms and a rooftop pool. Though small, the rooms are comfortable – book one on the fifth floor where there are tiny balconies with lovely views over the rooftops of the city.

ME Madrid Reina Victoria

MAP P5 ■ Plaza de Santa Ana 14 ■ 912 76 47 47 ■ www.melia.com ■ €€

Refurbishments have converted this beautiful early 1900s building into a modern hotel with great facilities and a trendy, penthouse bar. The hotel is a much-loved landmark, located conveniently close to Puerta del Sol and the city's museums.

Palacio PL Conde de Miranda

MAP L5 ■ Plaza del Conde de Miranda 1 ■ 900 37 39 78 ■ www.palacioplconde demiranda.com ■ €€

Each apartment in this accommodation is indiv-idually decorated and draws inspiration from famous couples, including Romeo and Juliet, Harry and Sally, Ross and Rachel and Popeye and Olive. Kitchens have a stocked fridge, a stove, oven, coffee machine and dishwasher. Babysitting services are also available.

Posada del Dragón

MAP L6 ■ Calle de la Cava Baja 14 ■ 911 19 14 24 ■ www.posadadeldragon. com ■ €€

Sections of medieval wall and an attractive wooden staircase are preserved in this 16th-century inn, but the guest rooms are entirely contemporary with their bold colours and modern lights and

furnishings. The trendy restaurant – one of many that line the Cava Baja – serves tasty local cuisine. It's a lively area so ask for a room at the back if you prefer a quiet night.

Room-Mate Alicia

MAP Q5 ■ Calle del Prado 2 ■ 913 89 60 95 ■ www. room-matehotels.com ■ €€€

This modern hotel, conveniently located in the Plaza de Santa Ana, is an ideal choice for those keen to enjoy Madrid's nightlife. The colourful rooms have large win-dows that look out over this vibrant square.

Hotel Único

MAP G2 ■ Calle de Claudio Coello 67 ■ 917 81 01 73 ■ www.unico hotelmadrid.com ■ €€€

An absolute favourite with the fashion crowd, this boutique hotel occupies a beautifully remodelled 19th-century mansion in upmarket Salamanca. There is a Michelin-starred restaurant with a charming garden. The hotel also has a personal shopper to tend to all your shopping requirements.

Only You Hotel

MAP E3 ■ Calle Barquillo 21 ■ 910 05 22 22 ■ www. onlyyouhotels.com ■ €€€

Catalan designer Lázaro Rosa-Violán is responsible for the striking decor at this hotel, which occupies a 19th-century mansion in the Chueca neighbour-hood. Many rooms have original beamed ceilings, which are paired with contemporary wallpaper and furnishings. Visitors can relax in the lounge bar, set in a former bookshop.

Business Hotels

Meliá Barajas

**Avenida de Logroño 305
■ 912 76 47 47 ■ www.
melia.com ■ €€**

On the approach road to Barajas airport, this 229-room hotel is convenient for the IFEMA Exhibition Centre. Rooms are comfortable and the facilities include a garden, outdoor pool, restaurants, gym, meeting rooms and a free airport shuttle.

NH Collection Palacio de Aranjuez

**MAP B1 ■ Calle de San Antonio 22, Aranjuez
■ 918 09 92 22 ■ www.
nh-collection.com ■ €**

This lovely hotel overlooks the Palace of Aranjuéz and offers reliable facilities for meetings and events. The superbly appointed rooms include espresso machines, satellite TV and WI-Fi. There is also a fitness centre and sauna.

AC-Aitana

**MAP B1 ■ Paseo de la Castellana 152 ■ 914 58 49 70 ■ www.marriott.
com ■ €€**

The facilities at this fully renovated 4-star business hotel include on-site parking, a restaurant and bar, reading room, fitness centre and two small conference rooms. All rooms are equipped with satellite TV, two phones and Wi-Fi.

Catalonia Gran Vía

**MAP R3 ■ Gran Vía 9 ■ 915 31 22 22 ■ www.catalonia
hotels.com ■ €€**

Conveniently situated, this comfortable hotel is also handy for sightseeing. The modern rooms offer satellite TV, and some

of the new rooms are equipped with jacuzzis. Facilities include a Catalan restaurant, a gym, a full-service spa and sauna.

Exe Moncloa

**MAP B1 ■ Calle Arcipreste Hita 10 ■ 917 45 92 99
■ www.hotelexemoncloa.
com ■ €€**

Located in front of the Intercambiador de Moncloa Metro and bus hub, this modern hotel offers a comfortable stay, with good facilities for business travellers. It also has a swimming pool.

Hotel H10 Tribeca

**MAP B1 ■ Calle de Pedro Teixeira 5 ■ 915 97 15 68
■ www.h10hotels.com
■ €**

This 4-star hotel is in an excellent location within Madrid's business district. Facilities include three meeting rooms, a private dining room and Wi-Fi.

Ilunion Suites

**Calle López de Hoyos 143
■ Metro Alfonso XIII ■ 917 44 50 00 ■ www.ilunion
suitesmadrid.com ■ €€**

North of the centre, this hotel has 120 suites, all equipped with satellite TV. Facilities include an international restaurant.

NH Madrid Ribera de Manzanares

**MAP OFF MAP AT B6
■ Paseo Virgen del Puerto 57 ■ 913 64 32 48 ■ www.
nh-hotels.com ■ €**

Overlooking the Manzanares River, this hotel offers value accommodation, plus 12 meeting rooms, a planning service for conferences and other events, and extras such as private parking, a gym, and a restaurant and bar.

Radisson Blu Prado Hotel Madrid

**MAP F5 ■ Calle Moratín 52 ■ 915 24 26 26
■ www.radissonblu.com
■ €€**

Offering large rooms with plenty of space in which to work, this sleekly designed hotel offers all the usual amenities for the business traveller, including meeting rooms and a business centre. Other amenities include a luxurious spa, a whisky bar and a superb location right opposite the Prado.

InterContinental Hotel

**MAP G1 ■ Paseo de la Castellana 49 ■ 917 00 73 00 ■ www.ihg.com
■ €€€**

A wide choice of meeting and conference rooms, a dedicated concierge team and excellent facilities including a 24-hour business centre have made this luxury hotel in Madrid's main financial district a winner with business travellers. Unwind in the 24-hour fitness centre or indulge in some spa pampering.

Budget Accommodation

B&B Hotel Las Rozas

**MAP B1 ■ Calle Perú 2
■ 916 30 17 17 ■ www.
hotel-bb.es ■ €**

Modern hotel set in Las Rozas, just a 30-minute drive from Madrid's centre and conveniently located for visiting the Sierra Norte of Madrid. Rooms of this hotel are large and airy, with free Wi-Fi service all throughout.

For a key to hotel price categories see p142

The Hat Madrid
MAP C5 ▪ Calle Imperial 9 ▪ 917 72 85 72 ▪ www.thehatmadrid.com ▪ €

The motto here is "Wherever I lay my hat, that's my home." This welcoming vibe runs throughout the hostel, which also offers private rooms with en suite bathrooms. Great breakfast buffet on the terrace, and there's a rooftop bar with amazing views.

Hostal Adis
MAP D3 ▪ Calle de la Puebla, 14 ▪ 915 31 56 44 ▪ www.hostaladismadrid.com ▪ €

Located just a few meters from the Gran Via and 10 minutes away from Puerta del Sol, this is a pleasant hotel with modern rooms equipped with LED TVs, central heating and Wi-Fi. Luggage storage is also available.

Hostal Gonzalo
MAP E5 ▪ Calle Cervantes 34, 3rd floor ▪ 914 29 27 14 ▪ www.hostalgonzalo.com ▪ €

A pleasant hostel in a historic part of Madrid, close to the museums of the Paseo del Prado. Some rooms have balconies overlooking a quiet residential street, bearing in mind that this area is known for its nightlife.

Hostal La Prensa
MAP M2 ▪ Gran Vía 46, 8° ▪ 915 31 93 07 ▪ www.hostallaprensa.com ▪ €

With views of the Gran Vía, this delightful guesthouse has cosy rooms decorated in colourful prints and all with air conditioning and private bathrooms. It's set in a skyscraper built in the 1920s.

Hostal Persal
MAP P5 ▪ Plaza del Angel 12 ▪ 913 69 46 43 ▪ www.hostalpersal.com ▪ €

Located overlooking a peaceful square, and yet surrounded by shops, bars and monuments, this hostel is excellent value. The comfortable rooms all have satellite TV and some overlook the courtyard. It also has its own coffee shop, which is a good place to get to know fellow guests and to trade information.

Lapepa Chic B&B
MAP F4 ▪ Plaza de las Cortes 4 ▪ 648 47 47 42 ▪ www.lapepa-bnb.com ▪ €

Just a stone's throw from Madrid's great trio of big museums, this B&B offers stylish rooms decorated in bright colours, and a cosy lounge with a kitchen corner where guests can gather for breakfast. Service is excellent and iPod docks are available.

Hotel Life
MAP M1 ▪ Calle Pizarro 16 ▪ 915 31 47 44 ▪ www.hotellifemadrid.es ▪ €€

The bright, modern rooms at this good value hotel feature original upcycled furnishings and art, and a mixture of contemporary and vintage decor. Convenient extras include free Wi-Fi and laptop hire, and the lively bars and cafés of the Malasaña district on the doorstep.

Mora
MAP F5 ▪ Paseo del Prado 32 ▪ 914 20 15 69 ▪ www.hotelmora.com ▪ €€

Art lovers on a budget should look no further than this modest-sized hotel, just across the road

from the Prado. Some rooms have views of the famous avenue. Room safes and satellite TV are other pluses. It's very popular, so book ahead.

TOC Hostel
MAP N4 ▪ Plaza Celenque 3-5 ▪ 915 32 13 04 ▪ www.tochostels.com ▪ €€

One of the new breed of designer hostels, this offers a choice of funkily decorated private guest rooms or dorms. Get to know your fellow travellers in the bar, or over a game of pool. Whip up some dinner in the well-equipped kitchen.

Hotels with a Difference

Box Art Hotel – La Torre
MAP A1 ▪ Paseo de los Rosales 48, Collado Mediano ▪ 918 55 85 58 ▪ www.latorreboxart hotel.es ▪ €

Nestled in the mountains, this is the perfect place to disconnect. Alongside its unique style, the hotel has a spa, sauna and outdoor pool, as well as bicycles for guest use and even cookery workshops. Navacerrada ski resort is just minutes away. Children aged 12 years and upwards are welcome.

Hotel Emperador
MAP L2 ▪ Gran Vía 53 ▪ 915 47 28 00 ▪ www.emperadorhotel.com ▪ €€

This hotel is in a great location overlooking Plaza de España. Its luxurious rooms (suites have their own Jacuzzis and hydro-massage showers) make it the first choice for many celebrities. There's also an expansive rooftop swimming pool with panoramic views.

NH Collection Madrid Eurobuilding

Calle Padre Damián 23 ▪ 913 53 73 00 ▪ www. nh-hotels.com ▪ €€
In Madrid's main business district, this glossy hotel has a huge LED-domed screen in the lobby, and its Living Lab guest rooms come with high-tech features such as ultra HD TVs and intelligent lighting. Rooms on the highest floors have breathtaking views, and dining options include DiverXO, Madrid's only restaurant with three Michelin stars.

Petit Palace Ópera

MAP M4 ▪ Calle Arenal 16 ▪ 915 64 43 55 ▪ www. petitpalaceopera.com ▪ €€
Madrid is slowly becoming more bike-friendly, and at this central hotel you can borrow bikes for free. The hotel also provides other handy freebies for the pocket-conscious traveller, such as the free use of an iPad and Mi-Fi (portable Wi-Fi). Families will appreciate the multi-bed rooms that sleep up to six, and the use of buggies and cots.

Eurostars Madrid Tower

Paseo de la Castellana 259 B ▪ 913 34 27 00 ▪ www.eurostarsmadrid tower.com ▪ €€
This hotel is set in the PwC Tower, which forms part of the Cuatro Torres business district, and it is one of the tallest buildings in Madrid. Enjoy breath-taking views from the pool in the spa and health club, or from the gastronomic Volvoreta restaurant on the 30th floor.

Hotel Atlántico

MAP N2 ▪ Gran Vía 38 ▪ 915 22 64 80 ▪ www. hotelatlantico.es ▪ €€€
This hotel is a favourite with guests, who keep coming back thanks to its comfortable, classically decorated rooms, its charming service and its fantastically central location. But the icing on the cake is without doubt the gorgeous rooftop terrace, where you can enjoy a drink and watch the sun set over the ancient rooftops of the historic city centre.

Puerta América

Avenida de América 41 ▪ 917 44 54 00 ▪ www. hotelpuertamerica.com ▪ €€€
The brainchild of French architect Jean Nouvel, this modern hotel is located on one of the main arteries into the centre of Madrid. Each of its 12 floors has been designed by a well-known architect or designer, including Norman Foster, Arata Isozaki, Zaha Hadid and Javier Mariscal. The hotel also has a good restaurant.

Room Mate Óscar

MAP Q2 ▪ Plaza de Pedro Zerolo 12 ▪ 917 01 11 73 ▪ https://room-matehotels.com ▪ €€€
Part of the popular Room Mate chain, this hotel has ultra-stylish, modern rooms decorated in vibrant colours, but the highlight is undoubtedly the rooftop sun deck and swimming pool. There's a poolside bar, and DJ sessions make it particularly popular on sultry summer nights.

Urso Hotel & Spa

MAP E2 ▪ Calle Mejía Lequerica 8 ▪ 914 44 44 58 ▪ hotelurso.com ▪ €€€
Spacious, fashionably decorated guest rooms, wonderful staff and a great full-service spa by Natura Bissé, complete with a small heated pool, make this ideal for a luxurious urban break. The best rooms have French doors leading out onto private terraces.

Vincci The Mint

MAP E4 ▪ Calle Gran Vía, 10 ▪ 912 03 06 50 ▪ www. vinccithemint.com ▪ €€€
As soon as you enter this enigmatic hotel, you are received with a drink at the reception. Gourmet à la carte breakfast is served all day, and coffee- tea machines are available in all rooms. Grab cocktails and snacks from the rooftop food-truck and enjoy the panoramic view.

VP El Jardín de Recoletos

MAP G3 ▪ Calle Gil de Santivanes 6 ▪ 917 81 16 40 ▪ www.recoletoshotel. com ▪ €€€
This hotel has a beautiful garden terrace, an oasis of green in the heart of the city. Comfortably furnished rooms are light and airy, and you can dine on traditional cuisine amid the magnolias and palm trees in the hotel's romantic restaurant.

For a key to hotel price categories see p142

General Index

Acknowledgments

This edition updated by

Contributor Marta Bescos
Senior Editor Alison McGill
Senior Designer Vinita Venugopal
Project Editors Dipika Dasgupta, Alex Pathe
Assistant Editor Anjasi N.N.
Editor Chhavi Nagpal
Picture Research Administrator Vagisha Pushp
Picture Research Manager Taiyaba Khatoon
Publishing Assistant Halima Mohammed
Jacket Designer Jordan Lambley
Senior Cartographer Subhashree Bharati
Cartography Manager Suresh Kumar
Senior DTP Designer Tanveer Zaidi
Senior Production Editor Jason Little
Senior Production Controller Samantha Cross
Deputy Managing Editor Beverly Smart
Managing Editors Shikha Kulkarni,
Hollie Teague
Managing Art Editor Sarah Snelling
Senior Managing Art Editor Priyanka Thakur
Art Director Maxine Pedliham
Publishing Director Georgina Dee

DK would like to thank the following for
their contribution to the previous editions:
Christopher Rice, Melanie Rice, Mary-Ann
Gallaghar, Hilary Bird.

The publisher would like to thank the
following for their kind permission to
reproduce their photographs:
Key: a-above; b-below/bottom; c-centre; f-far;
l-left; r-right; t-top

Alamy Stock Photo: agefotostock 23cr, 88tl,
93cr, / Artelan 34clb, / María Galán 97crb, / David
Miranda 96br, 101tr, / Guillermo Navarro 57crb, /
José Ramiro 73clb / Lucas Vallecillos 25tl; Peter
Barritt 20tl; Ian Dagnall 80b; Emma Durnford
115cr; Factofoto 59br, 94c; Kevin Foy 63tl; María
Galán 112clb; geogphotos 120br; Kevin George
58tl; Steve Hamblin 14tr; Hemis 14br; Heritage
Image Partnership Ltd 18br; Phil Hill 91cr;
Peter Horree 38cl, 90bl, 108tr; INTERFOTO/
Monasterio de Las Descalzas Reales, Madrid *La
Dolorosa*, by Pedro de Mena 100tl, /Museo del
Prado, Madrid *The Adoration of the Shepherds*
(1612) by El Greco 16clb; JOHN KELLERMAN
79bl; Stefano Politi Markovina 51tr; Masterpics/
Prado Museum *Carlos III* (1761) by Anton Rafael
Mengs 15tl, /Prado Museum *Self Portrait* (1498)
by Albrecht Durer 21tl, /Prado Museum *Autodafe
on Plaza Mayor with Charles II* (1680) by Francisco
Rizi 46t; Melba Photo Agency 59tl; North Wind
Picture Archives 46cb; PjrTravel 26cl; PjrTravel
70br; Prisma Archivo 84cb, *Battle of Turin, 1706*
by Joseph Parrocel 15b; RosalreneBetancourt 6
88crb; ruelleruelle 86cr; 122t; SAGAPHOTO.
COM/Patrick Forget 118tl; Alex Segre 125tl;
Sueddeutsche Zeitung Photo/Giribas Jose
65cra; Lucas Vallecillos 124br; World History
Archive 35tl; Zoonar GmbH 72c, 95bl.

Jamones Julián Becerro: 113br.

El Bocaito: 67cla.

Bridgeman Images: De Agostini Picture
Library 14cl; Museo Lazaro Galdiano, Madrid
The Adoration of the Magi (1567-70) by El Greco
(Domenico Theotocopuli) 85tr; Prado, Madrid
Las Meninas or The Family of Philip IV (c.1656)
by Diego Rodriguez de Silva y Velazquez 16br.

Café de Oriente: 105clb.

Capas Seseña: 70clb.

Casa Alberto: 117cr.

Casa Museo Sorolla: *Walk by the Sea* (1909)
by Joaquin Sorolla 49cr; *The Horse's Bath*
(1909) by Joaquín Sorolla 87bl.

Casa Patas: 115tc.

Corbis: Arcaid/Richard Bryant 13tl; Eye
Ubiquitous/Bennett Dean 112tr; The Gallery
Collection 18tl; Hemis/René Mattes 41tl;
Leemage/Prado Museum *The Spinners or
The Fable of Arachne* (c.1657) by Diego
Velazquez 17tl.

Dreamstime.com: Alezia 10br; Anibaltrejo
92tl; Bpperry 10cr, 109bl; Btlife 25crb; Dennis
Dolkens 6tl, 56t; Dinozzaver 107tr; Epalaciosan
95tl; Gil7416 52t; Gilles Gaonach 2tl, 8-9;
Gregory108 54-5; Hect 51cl; Hemeroskopion
75tr; David Herraez 60tl; Icconiac 72t; Jackf
127tl; Lestertairpolling 123cra; Lukasz Janyst
128-9tc; Javierespuny 7cr; Justinmetz 37cr;
Karsol 129bc; Lawmoment 74bl; Macsim 40-1;
Andres Garcia Martin 4b, 11cr; Miff32 4crb;
Milosk50 121clb; Carlos Mora 75clb; Mtrommer
127br; Nikolais 80tr; Outsiderzone 37tl, 126tl;
Pabkov 41cr, 53br; Paha_l 36br; Narcis Parfenti
128cl; William Perry 10bl; Jozef Sedmak 24cr;
Sedmak 78tl, 102tr; Siempreverde22 12-13;
Slowcentury 26br, 106tl; Andreas Steidlinger
67cla; Tomas1111 3tl, 76-7; Tupungato 73clb,
97cla; Vwalakte 7tr.

El Buda Feliz: Cali Bibang 99tl .

Getty Images: DeAgostini 43b; Pablo Blazquez
Dominguez 28bl; Hulton Archive 43tl, /Culture
Club 47clb; Daniel Hernanz Ramos 24bl; Rafa
Samano 47br; UIG/MyLoupe 90tc.

Hotel ME Madrid: Radio 116br.

iStockphoto.com: fotoVoyager 26-7c,
JJFarquitectos 36-7c; LucVi 1; miralex 22-3c;
SeanPavonePhoto 4t; TkKurikawa 114bl.

Licores Madrueño S.L.: 71cl.

Madrid Destino: Sofía Menendez 79t.

Manuel Gonzalez Contreras: 70cra.

Mercado de San Miguel: 105br.

Meson Cuevas Del Vino: 110cr.

© Museo Thyssen-Bornemisza, Madrid: 11t;
Young Knight in a Landscape (1510) by Vittore
Carpaccio 28bl; *Swaying Dancer* (1877-9) by
Edgar Degas 30bc; *Christ and Woman of Samaria
at the Well* (1310-1) by Duccio di Buoninsegna
28-9; *The Annunciation* (c.1567-1577) by El Greco
29crb; *Portrait of Henry VIII of England* (1537) by
Hans Holbein The Younger 29tc; *Hotel Room*
(1931) by Edward Hopper 31br; *Still Life with
Instruments* (1915) by Liubov Popova 31tl;
Woman with a Parasol in a Garden (c.1873)
by Pierre-Auguste Renoir 30tl.

Museo Arqueologico Nacional: Santiago
Relanzón 38bc, 38-9, 39tl, 39ca, 39cb, 39b.

Museo Cerralbo: Latova José Fernández-Luna 48t.

Museo Chicote: Emilia Brandao 64t, emiliabrandaophoto 98bl.

Museo del Romanticismo: Pablo Linés Viñuales 119tr.

Museo Nacional Centro de Arte Reina Sofía: Joaquín Cortes/ Roman Lores 11tr; *Retrato II* (1938) by Joan Miro © Successió Miró/ADAGP, Paris and DACS London 2016 33cr; *Guernica* (1937) by Pablo Picasso © Succession Picasso/ DACS, London 2016 35b; *Accidente Also known as Self-portrait* (1936) by Alfonso Ponce de León 33tr; *Le tertulia del Cafe de Pombo* (1920) by Jose Gutierrez Solana © DACS 2016 32bl.

NH Hoteles/Estado Puro: Gonzalo Arche 69clb.

Palacio de Cibeles: 83c.

La Parra: 131br.

Ramses Life: 65bl.

Reserva y Cata: Leonardo Castro 123clb.

Restaurante Botín: 68t.

Restaurante Horcher: 83bl.

Robert Harding Picture Library: Hugo Alonso 110-1; Barbara Boensch 2tr, 44-5; Jeremy Bright 37crb; Adrian Dominguez 4cl; Elan Fleisher 3tr,132-3; Juergen Richter 11b, 12crb; Arturo Rosas 4cr; White Star/ Monica Gumm 4clb, / Alberto Mateo 32-3.

Shutterstock.com: F. J. CARNEROS 103bl.

SuperStock: age fotostock 10cla, 40br, 120tl; Album/Joseph Martin 16-7; Classic Vision/age fotostock/Museo de la Real Academia de Bellas Artes de San Fernando *Self-portrait Goya at 69 years of age* by Francisco de Goya y Lucientes 19tl; Fine Art Images/Museo del Prado *The Third of May 1808* (1814) by Francisco de Goya 19b, *The Three Graces* (16350 by Pieter Paul Rubens, c. 20bc, *Parnassus* (1631) by Nicolas Poussin 21b; Joseph Martin 10cl; Peter Barritt 40cl, 42tc; Travel Library Limited 11cb.

Taberna de Antonio Sanchez: 66b, Picasa117cb.

Taberna del Alabardero: 66cl.

Teatro Real: Javier del Real 62b, 102bl.

La Violeta: 113tc.

Xanadu: 61cla.

Cover

Front and spine: **iStockphoto.com:** LucVi 1.
Back: **Alamy Stock Photo:** María Galán cl; **Dreamstime.com:** Erix2005 crb, Konstantin Kopachinskii tl, Sean Pavone tr; **iStockphoto. com:** LucVi b.

Pull Out Map Cover

iStockphoto.com: LucVi.
All other images © Dorling Kindersley
For further information see www.dkimages.com

Commissioned Photography: Barnabas Kindersley, Lisa Linder, Rough Guides/Ian Aitken, Rough Guides/Tim Draper, Rough Guides/Lydia Evans, Kim Sayer, Clive Streeter, John Whittaker, Peter Wilson.

Illustrator: Chris Orr & Associates.

Penguin Random House

First Edition 2003
Published in Great Britain by
Dorling Kindersley Limited
DK, One Embassy Gardens, 8 Viaduct
Gardens, London SW11 7BW, UK

The authorised representative in the EEA is
Dorling Kindersley Verlag GmbH. Arnulfstr.
124, 80636 Munich, Germany

Published in the United States by
DK Publishing, 1745 Broadway, 20th Floor,
New York, NY 10019, USA

Copyright © 2003, 2023
Dorling Kindersley Limited
A Penguin Random House Company
23 24 25 26 10 9 8 7 6 5 4 3 2 1

All rights reserved.

A CIP catalogue record is available from the British Library.

A catalogue record for this book is available from the Library of Congress.

ISSN 1479-344X
ISBN 978-0-2416-1593-5
Printed and bound in Malaysia

www.dk.com

As a guide to abbreviations in visitor information blocks: **Adm** = admission charge; **D** = dinner; **L** = lunch.

Phrase Book

In an Emergency

Help!	¡Socorro!	soh-koh-roh
Stop!	¡Pare!	pah-reh
Call…	¡Llame a…	yah-meh ah
…a doctor!	…un médico!	oon meh-dee-koh
…an ambulance!	…una ambulancia!	oonah ahm-boo-lahn-thee-ah
…the police!	…la policía!	lah poh-lee-thee-ah
…the fire brigade!	…los bomberos!	lohs bohm-beh-rohs

Where is…	¿Dónde está…	dohn-deh ehs-tah
…the nearest hospital?	…el hospital más próximo?	ehl ohs peet-tahl mahs prohx-ee-moh

Communication Essentials

Yes	Sí	see
No	No	noh
Please	Por favor	pohr fah-vohr
Thank you	Gracias	grah-thee-ahs
Excuse me	Perdone	pehr-doh-neh
Hello	Hola	oh-lah
Goodbye	Adiós	ah-dee-ohs
Good night	Buenas noches	bweh-nahs noh-chehs
Morning	La mañana	lah mah-nyah-nah
Afternoon/Evening	La tarde	lah tahr-deh
Yesterday	Ayer	ah-yehr
Today	Hoy	oy
Tomorrow	Mañana	mah-nya-nah
Here	Aquí	ah-kee
There	Allí	ah-yee
What?	¿Qué?	keh
When?	¿Cuándo?	kwahn-doh
Why?	¿Por qué?	pohr-keh
Where?	¿Dónde?	dohn-deh

Useful Phrases

How are you?	¿Cómo está usted?	koh-moh ehs-tah oos-tehd
Very well, thank you	Muy bien, gracias	mwee bee-ehn grah-thee-ahs
Pleased to meet you.	Encantado de conocerle.	ehn-kahn-tah-doh deh thehr-leh
See you soon	Hasta pronto	ahs-tah-prohn-toh
That's fine	Está bien	ehs-tah bee-ehn
Where is/are…?	¿Dónde está/están…?	dohn-deh ehs-tah/ehs-tahn
How far is it to…?	Cuántos metros/ kilómetros hay de aquí a…?	kwahn-tohs meh-trohs/kee-loh-meh-trohs eye deh ah-kee ah
Which way to…?	¿Por dónde se va a…?	pohr dohn-deh seh bah ah
Do you speak English?	¿Habla inglés?	ah-blah een-glehs
I don't understand	No comprendo	noh kohm-prehn-doh
Could you speak more slowly please?	¿Puede hablar más despacio por favor?	pweh-deh ah-blahr mahs dehs-pah-thee-oh pohr fah-vohr
I'm sorry	Lo siento	loh see-ehn-toh

Useful Words

big	grande	grahn-deh
small	pequeño	peh-keh-nyoh
hot	caliente	kah-lee-ehn-teh
cold	frío	free-oh
good	bueno	bweh-noh
bad	malo	mah-loh
well	bien	bee-ehn
open	abierto	ah-bee-ehr-toh
closed	cerrado	thehr-rah-doh
left	izquierda	eeth-key-ehr-dah
right	derecha	deh-reh-chah
straight on	todo recto	toh-doh rehk-toh
near	cerca	thehr-kah
far	lejos	leh-hohs

up	arriba	ah-ree-bah
down	abajo	ah-bah-hoh
early	temprano	tehm-prah-noh
late	tarde	tahr-deh
entrance	entrada	ehn-trah-dah
exit	salida	sah-lee-dah
toilet	servicios	sehr-bee-thee-ohs
more	más	mahs
less	menos	meh-nohs

Shopping

How much does this cost?	¿Cuánto cuesta esto?	kwahn-toh kwehs-tah ehs-toh
I would like…	Me gustaría…	meh goos-ta-ree-ah
Do you have Wi-Fi?	¿Tiene Wi-Fi?	tee-yeh-nehn Wee-Fee
Do you take cards?	¿Aceptan tarjetas?	ah-thehp-tahn tahr-heh-tahs
What time do you open/close?	¿A qué hora abren/cierran?	ah keh oh-rah ah-brehn/thee-ehr-rahn
This one	Éste	ehs-teh
That one	Ése	eh-seh
expensive	caro	kahr-oh
cheap	barato	bah-rah-toh
size, clothes	talla	tah-yah
size, shoes	número	noo-mehr-oh
antiques shop	la tienda de antigüedades	tee-ehn-dah dah ahn-tee-gweh-dah-dehs
bakery	la panadería	pah-nah-deh ree-ah
bank	el banco	bahn-koh
bookshop	la librería	lee-breh-ree-ah
cake shop	la pastelería	pahs-teh-leh-ree-ah
chemist's	la farmacia	ahr-mah-thee-ah
market	el mercado	mehr-kah-doh
newsagent's	el kiosko de prensa	kee-ohs-koh deh prehn-sah
post office	la oficina de correos	oh-fee-thee-nah deh kohr-reh-ohs
shoe shop	la zapatería	thah-pah-teh-ree-ah
supermarket	el super-mercado	soo-pehr-mehr-kah-doh
travel agency	la agencia de viajes	ah-hehn-thee-ah -deh beeah-hehs

Sightseeing

art gallery	el museo de arte	moo-seh-oh deh ahr-teh
cathedral	la catedral	kah-teh-drahl
church	la iglesia, la basílica	ee-gleh-see-ah bah-see-lee-kah
garden	el jardín	hahr-deen
library	la biblioteca	bee-blee-oh-teh-kah
museum	el museo	moo-seh-oh
tourist information office	la oficina de turismo	oh-fee-thee-nah deh too-rees-moh
town hall	el ayunta-miento	ah-yoon-toh mee-ehn-toh
bus station	la estación de autobuses	ehs-tah-thee-ohn deh owtoh-boo-sehs
railway station	la estación de trenes	ehs-tah-thee-ohn deh treh-nehs

Staying in a Hotel

Do you have a vacant room?	¿Tiene una habitación libre?	tee-eh-neh oo-nah ah-bee-tah-thee-ohn lee-breh
double room	habitación doble	ah-bee-tah-thee-ohn doh-bleh
with double bed	con cama de matrimonio	kohn kah-mah deh mah-tree-moh-nee-oh
twin room	habitación con dos camas	ah-bee-tah-thee-ohn kohn dohs kah-mahs
single room	habitación individual	ah-bee-tah-thee-ohn een-dee-vee-doo-ahl

room with a bath	habitación con baño	ah-bee-tah-thee-ohn kohn bah-nyoh
porter	el botones	boh-toh-nehs
key	la llave	yah-veh
I have a reservation	Tengo una habitación reservada	tehn-goh oo-na ah-bee-tah-thee-ohn reh-sehr-bah-dah

Eating Out

Have you got a table for…?	¿Tiene mesa para…?	tee-eh-neh meh-sah pah-rah
I want to reserve a table	Quiero reservar una mesa	kee-eh-roh reh-sehr-bahr oo-nah meh-sah
The bill	La cuenta	kwehn-tah
I am vegetarian	Soy vegetariano/a	soy beh-heh-tah-ree-ah-no/na
I am vegan	Soy vegano	soy veh-gah-no
waitress/ waiter	camarera/ camarero	kah-mah-reh-rah/ kah-mah-reh-rroh
menu	la carta	kahr-tah
fixed-price menu	menú del día	meh-noo dehl dee-ah
wine list	la carta de vinos	kahr-tah deh bee-nohs
glass	un vaso	bah-soh
bottle	una botella	boh-teh-yah
knife	un cuchillo	koo-chee-yoh
fork	un tenedor	teh-neh-dohr
spoon	una cuchara	koo-chah-rah
breakfast	el desayuno	deh-sah-yoo-noh
lunch	la comida/ el almuerzo	koh-mee-dah/ ahl-mwehr-thoh
dinner	la cena	theh-nah
main course	el primer plato	pree-mehr plah-toh
starters	los entremeses	ehn-treh-meh-ses
dish of the day	el plato del día	plah-toh dehl dee-ah
coffee	el café	kah-feh
rare (meat)	poco hecho	poh-koh eh-choh
medium	medio hecho	meh-dee-oh eh-choh
well done	muy hecho	mwee eh-choh

Menu Decoder

al horno	ahl ohr-noh	baked
asado	ah-sah-doh	roast
el aceite	ah-thee-eh-teh	oil
las aceitunas	ah-theh-toon-ahs	olives
el agua mineral	ah-gwa mee-neh-rahl	mineral water
sin gas/con gas	seen gas/kohn gas	still/sparkling
el ajo	ah-hoh	garlic
el arroz	ahr-rohth	rice
el azúcar	ah-thoo-kahr	sugar
la carne	kahr-neh	meat
la cebolla	theh-boh-yah	onion
el cerdo	therh-doh	pork
la cerveza	thehr-beh-thah	beer
el chocolate	choh-koh-lah-teh	chocolate
el chorizo	choh-ree-thoh	spicy sausage
el cordero	kohr-deh-rroh	lamb
frito	free-toh	fried
la fruta	froo-tah	fruit
los frutos secos	froo-tohs seh-kohs	nuts
las gambas	gahm-bahs	prawns
el helado	eh-lah-doh	ice cream
el huevo	oo-eh-voh	egg
el jamón serrano	hah-mohn sehr-rah-noh	cured ham
la langosta	lahn-gohs-tah	lobster
la leche	leh-cheh	milk
el limón	lee-mohn	lemon
la mantequilla	mahn-teh-kee-yah	butter
la manzana	mahn-thah-nah	apple
los mariscos	mah-rees-kohs	seafood
la naranja	nah-rahn-hah	orange
el pan	pahn	bread
el pastel	pahs-tehl	cake

las patatas	pah-tah-tahs	potatoes
el pescado	pehs-kah-doh	fish
la pimienta	pee-mee-yehn-tah	pepper
el plátano	plah-tah-noh	banana
el pollo	poh-yoh	chicken
el postre	pohs-treh	dessert
el queso	keh-soh	cheese
la sal	sahl	salt
la salsa	sahl-sah	sauce
seco	seh-koh	dry
el solomillo	soh-loh-mee-yoh	sirloin
la sopa	soh-pah	soup
la tarta	tahr-tah	pie/cake
el té	teh	tea
la ternera	tehr-neh-rah	beef
el vinagre	bee-nah-greh	vinegar
el vino blanco	bee-noh blahn-koh	white wine
el vino rosado	bee-noh oh-sah-doh	rosé wine
el vino tinto	bee-noh een-toht	red wine

Numbers

0	cero	theh-roh
1	uno	oo-noh
2	dos	dohs
3	tres	trehs
4	cuatro	kwa-troh
5	cinco	theen-koh
6	seis	says
7	siete	see-eh-teh
8	ocho	oh-choh
9	nueve	nweh-veh
10	diez	dee-ehth
11	once	ohn-theh
12	doce	doh-theh
13	trece	treh-theh
14	catorce	kah-tohr-theh
15	quince	keen-theh
16	dieciséis	dee-eh-thee-seh-ees
17	diecisiete	dee-eh-thee-see-eh-teh
18	dieciocho	dee-eh-thee-oh-choh
19	diecinueve	dee-eh-thee-nweh-veh
20	veinte	beh-een-teh
21	veintiuno	beh-een-tee-oo-noh
22	veintidós	beh-een-tee-dohs
30	treinta	treh-een-tah
31	treinta y uno	treh-een-tah ee oo-noh
40	cuarenta	kwah-rehn-tah
50	cincuenta	theen-kwehn-tah
60	sesenta	seh-sehn-tah
70	setenta	seh-tehn-tah
80	ochenta	oh-chehn-tah
90	noventa	noh-vehn-tah
100	cien	thee-ehn
101	ciento uno	thee-ehn-toh oo-noh
200	doscientos	dohs-thee-ehn-tohs
500	quinientos	khee-nee-ehn-tohs
700	setecientos	seh-teh-thee-ehn-tohs
900	novecientos	noh-veh-thee-ehn-tohs
1,000	mil	meel

Time

one minute	un minuto	oon mee-noo-toh
one hour	una hora	oo-na oh-rah
half an hour	media hora	meh-dee-a oh-rah
Monday	lunes	loo-nehs
Tuesday	martes	mahr-tehs
Wednesday	miércoles	mee-ehr-koh-lehs
Thursday	jueves	hoo-weh-vehs
Friday	viernes	bee-ehr-nehs
Saturday	sábado	sah-bah-doh
Sunday	domingo	doh-meen-goh

Street Index